the series on schoo.. .

Patricia A. Wasley
University
of Washington

Ann Lieberman
Senior Scholar,
Stanford University

Joseph P. McDonald
New York
University

SERIES EDITORS

The Networked Teacher: How New Teachers Build
Social Networks for Professional Support
KIRA J. BAKER-DOYLE

How Teachers Become Leaders:
Learning from Practice and Research
ANN LIEBERMAN & LINDA D. FRIEDRICH

Peer Review and Teacher Leadership:
Linking Professionalism and Accountability
JENNIFER GOLDSTEIN

Improving the Odds: Developing Powerful Teaching
Practice and a Culture of Learning in Urban High Schools
THOMAS DEL PRETE

The Mindful Teacher
ELIZABETH MACDONALD & DENNIS SHIRLEY

Going to Scale with New School Designs:
Reinventing High School
JOSEPH P. MCDONALD, EMILY J. KLEIN, & MEG RIORDAN

Managing to Change: How Schools Can Survive
(and Sometimes Thrive) in Turbulent Times
THOMAS HATCH

Teacher Practice Online: Sharing Wisdom, Opening Doors
DÉSIRÉE H. POINTER MACE

Teaching the Way Children Learn
BEVERLY FALK

Teachers in Professional Communities:
Improving Teaching and Learning
ANN LIEBERMAN & LYNNE MILLER, EDS.

Looking Together at Student Work, 2nd Ed.
TINA BLYTHE, DAVID ALLEN, &
BARBARA SCHIEFFELIN POWELL

The Power of Protocols:
An Educator's Guide to Better Practice, 2nd Ed.
JOSEPH P. MCDONALD, NANCY MOHR, ALAN DICHTER, &
ELIZABETH C. MCDONALD

Schools-within-Schools:
Possibilities and Pitfalls of High School Reform
VALERIE E. LEE & DOUGLAS D. READY

Seeing Through Teachers' Eyes:
Professional Ideals and Classroom Practices
KAREN HAMMERNESS

Building School-Based Teacher Learning Communities:
Professional Strategies to Improve Student Achievement
MILBREY MCLAUGHLIN & JOAN TALBERT

Mentors in the Making:
Developing New Leaders for New Teachers
BETTY ACHINSTEIN & STEVEN Z. ATHANASES, EDS.

Community in the Making: Lincoln Center Institute, the
Arts, and Teacher Education
MADELEINE FUCHS HOLZER & SCOTT NOPPE-BRANDON, EDS.

Holding Accountability Accountable:
What Ought to Matter in Public Education
KENNETH A. SIROTNIK, ED.

Mobilizing Citizens for Better Schools
ROBERT F. SEXTON

The Comprehensive High School Today
FLOYD M. HAMMACK, ED.

The Teaching Career
JOHN I. GOODLAD & TIMOTHY J. MCMANNON, EDS.

Beating the Odds:
High Schools as Communities of Commitment
JACQUELINE ANCESS

At the Heart of Teaching: A Guide to Reflective Practice
GRACE HALL MCENTEE, JON APPLEBY, JOANNE DOWD,
JAN GRANT, SIMON HOLE, & PEGGY SILVA, WITH
JOSEPH W. CHECK

Teaching Youth Media: A Critical Guide to Literacy,
Video Production, and Social Change
STEVEN GOODMAN

Inside the National Writing Project:
Connecting Network Learning and Classroom Teaching
ANN LIEBERMAN & DIANE WOOD

Standards Reform in High-Poverty Schools:
Managing Conflict and Building Capacity
CAROL A. BARNES

Standards of Mind and Heart:
Creating the Good High School
PEGGY SILVA & ROBERT A. MACKIN

Upstart Startup:
Creating and Sustaining a Public Charter School
JAMES NEHRING

One Kid at a Time:
Big Lessons from a Small School
ELIOT LEVINE

Guiding School Change:
The Role and Work of Change Agents
FRANCES O'CONNELL RUST & HELEN FREIDUS, EDS.

Teachers Caught in the Action:
Professional Development That Matters
ANN LIEBERMAN & LYNNE MILLER, EDS.

(Continued)

the series on school reform, *continued*

The Networked Teacher

HOW NEW TEACHERS BUILD SOCIAL NETWORKS FOR PROFESSIONAL SUPPORT

KIRA J. BAKER-DOYLE

FOREWORD BY
ANN LIEBERMAN

TEACHERS
COLLEGE
PRESS

Teachers College
Columbia University
New York and London

Published by Teachers College Press, 1234 Amsterdam Avenue, New York, NY 10027

.

Library of Congress Cataloging-in-Publication Data

Baker-Doyle, Kira J.
  The networked teacher : how new teachers build social networks for professional support / Kira J. Baker-Doyle ; foreword by Ann Lieberman.
      p. cm. — (the series on school reform)
  Includes bibliographical references and index.
  ISBN 978-0-8077-5251-7 (pbk. : alk. paper) 1. Professional learning communities. 2. Teachers—Professional relationships. 3. Teachers—In-service training. 4. Teachers—Social networks. I. Title.
  LB1775.B325 2011
  370.71'1—dc23

                                                            2011024086

ISBN 978-0-8077-5251-7 (paperback)

Printed on acid-free paper
Manufactured in the United States of America

  18   17   16   15   14   13   12   11   8   7   6   5   4   3   2   1

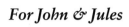

For John & Jules

Contents

Foreword

With all the talk about Facebook, LinkedIn, Ning, and blogs, it is wonderfully refreshing to read *The Networked Teacher: How New Teachers Build Social Networks for Professional Support,* because Baker-Doyle not only teaches us about where all this new technological knowledge came from and what it means, but she also uses the idea of social networks to study four beginning teachers in their first year to see its relevance. Each of the teachers, in their own way, stay afloat as a novice, while reaching out to experienced teachers, the principal, their family, parents, and more in different ways. And the differences matter!

We learn about *Intentional Professional Networks* (those people with whom the teachers interact and collaborate to solve professional problems) and *Diverse Professional Allies* (nontraditional support providers, such as parents, volunteers, students, and community members). Both provide support, sustenance, and knowledge for the novice teachers. Most importantly, we learn about the characteristics of support from these networks that had a profound influence on their teaching and learning during their first year.

The book reads like a great detective story as we learn about Michael, who is unsure about who to trust and, in the process of getting to know people in his school, isolates himself and feels unsupported; and about Maria, who is enthusiastic and outgoing and reaches out to a number of veteran teachers, who she claims as her "family." Steven connects to parents who, in their way, help him see how much they care about their kids; Susan joins a community-based choir, which turns out to be central to her growth during the first year.

From this work, we learn the real restrictions of mandated curriculum, test-oriented school cultures, as well as about schools that value co-teaching, after school clubs, and a wide variety of supports. Any and all of these characteristics of schools provide greater and lesser opportunities for new teachers to learn from and with their peers.

In short, social networking becomes a critical component for the success of novice teachers, for their pedagogical learning, their emotional sustenance, and their initiation into the teaching profession. While Facebook connects friends together, social networks connect novice teachers to their support systems that are necessary for their ongoing learning about teaching, curriculum, students, parents, the community, and the culture of their school. This book is a treat to read, as Baker-Doyle is at home with social networking, teaching, and the culture of schools, which makes the book a wonderful addition to reform literature and to our education of novice teachers.

Ann Lieberman

Acknowledgments

I would like to share my deepest thanks and respect for all of those who encouraged, supported, and pushed me to write this book. I would not have even thought it was possible without Ann Lieberman, whose belief in me and this project convinced me to take the leap—and I'm so glad I did! Thank you, Ann, for your help, feedback, mentoring, and constant reassurance along the way.

Much of this book comes from my previous research on teachers' social networks. There are many people to thank who inspired me, kept me questioning, and looking for answers. First I must thank Kathy Schultz, my former advisor and constant friend—I will miss our chats over coffee now that she is on the other side of the country, but there is always Skype! Another equally important friend, mentor, and collaborator is Susan Yoon, whose passion and energy constantly inspire me. The friends I developed as a graduate student at the University of Pennsylvania when I began this journey years ago continue to support me and are models of social justice educators and advocates: Ed Brockenbrough, Rob Connor, Cheryl Jones-Walker, Traci English-Clarke, Anita Chikkatur, and (then program-coordinator) Paul Skilton-Sylvester.

I wish I could thank the teachers that allowed me to come into their classrooms and ask them about their lives and work by name; alas, they are given pseudonyms here, but they know who they are—thank you to "Maria," "Michael," "Susan," and "Steven" for your generosity and openness.

As a teacher and graduate student my involvement in the Philadelphia Teachers' Learning Cooperative was a catalyst for my research and an inspiration to my practice. I would like to especially thank Lynne Strieb (who educated me in 1st and 2nd grade and continues to educate me through my life), as well as Betsy Wice, Helen Lamont, Susan Shapiro, and Lisa Hantman. Two very special individuals helped me not only through teaching but also through parenthood, work, and life—Anne Burns Thomas and Christina Puntel. These two amazing teachers are what teacher inquiry and social justice education are all about.

More recently I have had the pleasure of working with some brilliant scholars of social networks, who continue to stir my interests and motivate me to push forward. Thank you to Alan Daly and Nienke Moolenaar for your many words of encouragement—I look forward to our future collaborations! Thank you also to Lauren Anderson—it's amazing that we found each other, and I'm excited for our collaborations too. Although we've only had the American Education Research Association Conferences (AERA) to learn more about each other's work, my enthusiastic conversations with Margaret Reil and Andrew Thomas have helped me immensely in my work.

Writing is a tough job, and I stayed sane through the help of my writing group: Catriona MacLeod, Wendy Green, Sarah Hobson, and Sonia Rosen. I want to give a special thank you to Sonia, who has collaborated with me through the years and been a steady friend all the while. Another person who spent a lot of time helping to get the book "just right" was Marie Ellen Lacarda at Teachers College Press—thank you for supporting my writing and my new ideas about technology.

The students, faculty, and administration at Penn State Berks have been very supportive of my research and work. I would like to particularly thank Belen Rodriguez, Paul Esqueda, David Bender, and Amy Marsh for your support of my research endeavors.

Finally, last, but certainly not least, I would like to thank my friends and family for their continual support, babysitting, suggestions, and general understanding of an academic's crazy life. I want to start by thanking my friend and fellow writer, Meredith Broussard, for her writing suggestions and motivational speeches. My lifelong friends Jessica Falcone, Liz Theoharis, and Sanam Roder have always been there for me and I love them dearly. Thank you also to my aunt and fellow academic, Paula Rabinowitz, who reminded me not to pathologize writing (that might be too late), and to my in-laws, Eleanor Lindberg, Beth and Justin Barsanti, who all work with children with care and love.

My mother and father, Judi Bernstein-Baker and Karl Baker, are models of hard work and dedication to social justice—thank you for believing in me and holding my hand when I needed help. My son Jules Doyle reminds me to laugh and read, which keep me happy. Finally, my deepest thanks go to my husband, John Doyle, who, through the highs and the lows, has always loved and supported me.

The Networked Teacher

CHAPTER 1

Teaching in the Network Society

To be a Networked Teacher is to be a person who understands the theory and research behind social networks and puts this knowledge into action. New teachers have perhaps the greatest need to be intentional in their networking. They need support from others to locate resources, information, new ideas, emotional support, and inspiration in their first year. Yet, they begin their year with little knowledge of their school communities and with few established relationships in their schools. In addition, many are bewildered at the thought of building networks of support with colleagues, administrators, or parents.

This book aims to uncover the ways that new teachers can seek support through social networks (face-to-face and online). It explains the research and theory behind social networks, describes what effective social networking looks like, and reveals common obstacles that new teachers face in establishing support networks. The stories of four teachers illustrate the complexities of network development and the significant impact that networks can have on teachers' lives. The stories and frameworks offered here challenge common conceptions of professional support, recognizing the roles that students, families, and community members can play in teachers' work. Finally, this book offers tools and action guides to help new teachers become intentional networkers (including a companion Web site with tools for online networking and collaboration). It is a resource not only for beginning teachers, but also for teacher educators, mentors, school administrators, and scholars who study teachers' social networks. In this era of the "network society" (Castells, 1996), we must all work to understand the whats, whys, and hows of networking and its impact on teaching—here is a beginning.

A SOCIAL NETWORK PERSPECTIVE

Many see the words "social network" and think immediately of technology and the Internet. However, social networks are not only important because of the rise of the Internet; in the last 10 years, many social scientists have begun to apply a Social Network Perspective to their research (Baker-Doyle,

2010). The most well-known approach to research on social networks is Social Network Analysis (SNA), the study of links between members in a social network. Over the past decade, business analysts, researchers of organizational dynamics, and even community activists have used SNA to learn about how social networks are formed, what resources exist in the networks, and how to strategically develop social networks that can garner more resources and new ideas (i.e., social capital).

The popularity of research on social networks has grown alongside the emergence of the "Network Society" because it allows scholars to examine this complex phenomenon from a relational perspective; instead of just looking at the entirety of a group and its characteristics, social network researchers look in a systematic way at how and why people relate to each other. Thus, social network scholars can understand trends in workplace retention, innovation, and leadership from the point of view of who is working with whom, and what kind of relationship or interactions they have.

New Teacher Support and Retention

Supporting and retaining new teachers has become a central issue for American public schools; one in two new teachers leave teaching in their first 5 years, often because of their school environment and lack of support (Ingersoll & Smith, 2004; Nieto, 2003). Echoing the rise of the network society, teacher networks, professional learning communities, and mentorship programs (all collaborative activities) have begun to be widely accepted as important forms of professional support, especially for new teachers in induction programs. However, despite the importance of these new forms of support, few researchers have examined these practices from a Social Network Perspective. Further, until now, we knew even less about who the new "millennial" teachers chose to rely on in the face of these new support structures, and what kinds of support they ultimately receive. In this book, I present a framework for examining the various forms of support that exist in new teachers' social support networks from a Social Network Perspective. I describe the stories of four teachers and how the characteristics of their support networks (and networking activities) had a profound effect on their teaching experience.

The Rise of Social Networks

The emerging centrality of social networks and networking to our lives is a societal phenomenon. The concept of consciously developing a social network has become ingrained in the ways we think about making friends, getting jobs, and managing businesses or organizations. Perhaps as a result, research on social networks has rapidly expanded in the last 10 years and has made important contributions to our knowledge about how to sustain and develop resources and support for individuals and organizations.

Social networks in our lives. Sociologist Manuel Castells popularized the term "Network Society" in the first volume of his trilogy on the information age (1996). Castells (2000) argues that this new era emerged not only because of the Internet but also because of globalization, new technological paradigms in scientific research, the increasing global influence of multinational organizations (such as the UN), and a new ecological awareness. Together, these forces have influenced the way we live, eat, work, and play. Indeed, they have reshaped our economy to what has now been termed the "knowledge economy." This new economy is driven by social networks; the ability to communicate and collaborate effectively across contexts is vital to businesses, organizations, communities of practice, and individuals, to survive and thrive (Cross, Parker, Prusak, & Borgatti, 2003).

An example of this shift toward the importance of networks in our lives is evident in the dynamics of many American workplaces. As a result of globalization and shifts in the economy, workers are less likely to stay in one job for many years; compared to 30 years ago, when many people expected to work in one place for most of their lives, the chances that they will do so now are far less likely. With less stability in the job market, workers tend to rely more strongly on their personal networks developed across time and contexts rather than simply their colleagues at work. Online personal networking programs (such as Facebook and MySpace), email, blogs, and cell phones have allowed people to stay in touch longer with these personal contacts and reinforced the increasingly important role of personal social networks in people's lives.

The Millennial generation (Americans born after 1980) has been quick to recognize the importance of maintaining ties to people in their personal network and has done so mainly through new technology (Wong & Wong, 2008). A consistent characterization of this age group is their ability to build social networks. This is related to another characteristic of the generation: career switching and job hopping. In addition to new teachers, many young professionals have the tendency to quickly move on to a new job if they are not satisfied with the way they are being treated (Safer, 2007). The more frequently these young professionals move from job to job, the more important their personal network becomes for their reputation, access to new information, and discovering new opportunities.

Social networks in research. Accordingly, the notion of developing social networks has become quite important to people over the last decade due to these societal changes. This concept is equally important to organizations, scholars, and businesses because of the ability of social networks to efficiently exchange knowledge, foster innovation, and support members in a flexible and dynamic fashion. In essence, social networks produce and maintain *social capital*. Whereas *human capital* is considered the knowledge and skills possessed by a person, and *cultural capital* is the social practices and ways of being that a person learns, *social capital* is "who you know"—the relationships and memberships one has in a community, and the possible resources derived from these relationships. Thus, theoretically, the more *social capital* that exists in a network, the more knowledge, access to resources, and potential for innovation the network or the network member has in the network.

Therefore, in recent years, scholars have been trying to learn about what characteristics of a social network foster the greatest amount of *social capital*. Until about 2000, there were generally two schools of thought about *social capital* and social networks. Some sociologists (Coleman, 1990; Putnam, 1995) argued that communities (networks) in which the individuals are closely interconnected and share many norms and practices build greater social capital. The other perspective on social capital came from scholars who use SNA. They, particularly Granovetter (1985, 2003), argued that social networks in which few people know each other well and members are diverse in views or backgrounds foster more *social capital*. Recently, a third view has emerged from social network researchers: Closely knit social networks can help sustain and maintain social capital, and loosely linked, diverse networks can help cultivate innovation and new social capital. The field of research on social networks is very active and is helping us to learn more about how to bring resources and support to a network or to individuals in a network.

Teacher networks, communities of practice, and professional support. The career-switching patterns of the Millennial generation teachers relate to retention issues facing public schools in the United States, which have been struggling to retain teachers (particularly new urban teachers) since the early 1990s (NCTAF, 2003). What was once thought of as a teacher shortage is now realized as a problem of attrition; while there are many new teachers entering the profession, too many more are leaving (Ingersoll & Smith, 2003). Teachers leave their schools and careers for many reasons—changes in the family, relocation, retirement—but what has made the pinhole in the bucket turn into a verifiable hole has been the exodus of teachers because of the school environment and lack of professional support (Darling-Hammond & Sykes, 2003). What is so terrible about the professional support and school environments that new teachers quit their jobs after only a few years on the job? Combined with the heightened pressure and expectations from increased accountability and standardization, the traditional "sink or swim" support and "egg-crate" teacher isolationism model does not work (Costigan, Crocco, & Zumwalt, 2004).

Recent research on the problem of teacher support and attrition has suggested that new forms of professional development that encourage teachers to work together in organized "communities of practice" through teacher networks, collaborations, and mentoring relationships improve teacher retention and quality (Darling-Hammond & McLaughlin, 1995; Feiman-Nemser, Schwille, Carver, & Yusko, 1999; Ingersoll & Smith, 2004; Lieberman, 2000). Further, the networks and communities that teachers build in schools are key mediating factors in determining the actual outcome of school reforms and in influencing teacher buy-in of new initiatives (Anderson, 2010; Bidwell & Yasumoto, 1999; Daly, Finnigan, & Bolivar, 2009; Frank, Zhao, & Borman, 2004; Moolenaar, 2010; Penuel, Riel, Krause, & Frank, 2009). Understanding who new teachers seek out for support in these communities, and the activities they engage in, helps us learn more about how to address issues of teacher support, retention, and school reform.

Organized Communities of Practice

Organized teacher communities of practice are a powerful source of a teacher's professional learning and socialization (Adams, 2000; Lieberman & Miller, 1999; Lieberman & Wood, 2003; Burns-Thomas, 2007). Formal teacher networks, professional learning communities, school/university collaborations on curriculum or research, partnerships with neighborhood youth programs, and teacher involvement with district or national activities (task forces, study groups, standard-setting bodies) are all examples of organized teacher communities of practice. A community of practice is a community of learners that develop shared norms and practices through their collective activities and experiences (Christiansen & Ramadevi, 2002; Hausman & Goldring, 2001; Lave & Wenger, 1991; Oakes, Franke, Quartz, & Rogers, 2002). Thus, teacher networks and professional learning communities help socialize and guide teachers to become active members of the professional community.

Organized teacher communities of practice, such as formal teacher networks, also have significant flexibility in responding to rapidly changing conditions (i.e., school reform) by helping teachers collectively work to understand a school policy and incorporate versions of the policy that works best for their students (Adams, 2000; Lieberman & Wood, 2003; Thomas, 2007b). Some teacher networks, such as the National Writing Project, have long histories of working alongside districts to help teachers participate actively in school reform efforts (Cochran-Smith & Lytle, 1993; Lieberman & Wood, 2003).

Informal Social Networks

Teachers also develop personal networks and communities of practice in a less formalized, organized fashion, through their own socializing efforts in the school (Anderson, 2010; Baker-Doyle & Yoon, 2010; Frank et al., 2004; McCormick, Fox, Carmichael, & Proctor, 2010; Penuel et al., 2009). Some of this less formal networking has also been found to be a significant determinant in the outcomes of school reform efforts. For example:

- Cynthia Coburn's studies on teacher sensemaking have highlighted the important role of informal teacher communities in making sense of new reading programs (Coburn, 2001, 2005).
- Daly and colleagues' network studies on school reform identified patterns of isolation and segregation between teachers, school administrators, and central administrators, which stalled efforts to implement the new reform (Daly et al., 2009).
- Spillane and colleagues' studies of teacher leadership through a network lens have revealed informal social mechanisms of leadership that exist outside of formal hierarchical structures that have a strong impact on school reforms (Spillane, Halverson, & Diamond, 2004).

The important role of organized teacher communities of practice in supporting the professional growth of new teachers and helping them navigate new policies, and the significant findings on the influence of informal networks in teachers' responses to school reforms, demonstrates the centrality of teachers' social networks in shaping their own experiences as well as their schools. However, the majority of recent studies have *not* considered how informal social networks of new teachers shape their professional growth and support. The research and frameworks presented in this book examine this topic and reveal how essential new teachers' social support networks are to their experiences, and identify characteristics of social networks and networking behavior that were most beneficial in providing professional support to first-year teachers.

SUPPORTING NEW TEACHERS THROUGH SOCIAL NETWORKS

In this book, I use a Social Network Perspective to examine the experiences of first-year teachers. I argue that learning about how to network for professional support and building a strong personal support network is important for all pre-service teachers to learn in their preparation programs and early career teachers to learn in induction programs. My argument and perspective are shaped by my work and research on the social support networks of first-year teachers in urban schools (Baker-Doyle, 2008; Baker-Doyle, in press). The perspectives and frameworks I describe are ultimately tools and concepts for educators, administrators, and teachers to use in learning about informal teacher networks and building support for new teachers.

I developed two frameworks to examine and compare the social support networks of new teachers and their experiences:

1. A framework for understanding the *types of support new teachers receive*, and
2. A framework for analyzing and comparing *support network characteristics*.

The first framework I call the *Continuum of New Teacher Support,* which characterizes the support that beginning teachers receive by several factors, such as frequency of support and conceptualizations of teacher work. I describe this framework, along with research on support in social networks in Chapter 2. My second framework, a Social Network Perspective on new teachers' personal networks of support, consists of two main concepts: *Intentional Professional Networks* and *Diverse Professional Allies.* Chapter 3 describes these networks and shares real-life examples of new teachers' informal support networks and the network patterns that frequently take shape in the first year.

The frameworks and examples reveal the individuals in a teacher's support network who offer the kinds of support that promote professional growth and commitment. A teacher's support network is not developed at the sole discretion of the teacher; the school policies and culture are important factors in shaping a new teacher's support network. New teachers tend to avoid formal support programs and mentors if their support focuses primarily on outcomes, like helping teachers to develop strategies to raise test scores; they seek help with questions that are specific to their experiences and search for mentors who will help them incorporate their own ideas into their curriculum. Further, schools that embrace a traditional professional culture, which pushes teachers to work in isolation rather than be collaborative, can also alter a new teacher's initial interests in collaborating. In Chapter 4, the descriptions of the schools of four first-year teachers will illustrate how traditionalist school cultures and testing paradigms can override many well-intentioned mentorship programs and make networking for support difficult for new teachers.

Teachers can, of course, be active in developing their support network. Those who develop networks composed of individuals who can offer the professional support that meets their needs can gain more social capital in school, a strong sense of professionalism, and more confidence in developing their curriculum. These types of networks are most often formed by collaborative partnerships between professional colleagues in their schools as well as critical relationships with "nonprofessional" individuals, such as classroom volunteers, students, and students' parents. In Chapter 5, I describe the stories of Michael and Maria, two new teachers at the same school, who had very different networks and networking characteristics with colleagues at their school. Through their stories, you can see the power of one type of network, the Intentional Professional Network, in new teachers' experiences. In Chapter 6, I describe the experiences of another two teachers, Susan and Steven, and how their networking with parents and community members provided support and insight into their teaching. In the final chapter, I suggest a range of strategies for new teachers to use to consciously and strategically develop support networks. The appendixes of this book include tools that teachers and mentors can use to study and develop support networks, and information on how to use the companion Web site, www.thenetworkedteacher.com, to extend conversations about networking and collaboration.

This book takes what we know about the importance of networks and developing communities of practice and makes it personal. It will force teachers to ask: What does my support network look like? How do I, as an individual, ensure that we have a community that supports us in our profession? How could my relationship with another individual help to sustain the larger community? In an age when our lives are consumed with the idea of social networking, this new view will help to connect our knowledge about new teacher support with the network perspectives and technologies that are increasingly part of our lives.

CHAPTER 2

Networking for Support: Frameworks for Understanding Teacher Support and Social Networks

On the first day of school, a new teacher typically enters the schoolhouse armed with a few pedagogical strategies, content knowledge on the subject she is about to teach, and some experience in guided teaching practice. Within the next few days, the teacher discovers an aspect of school that she didn't learn about in her teacher education program—the social and political dynamics of school. Pre-service teachers often leave their teacher preparation programs with little understanding of the role of collegial relationships and school politics in their teaching experience, or how to negotiate the politics or develop effective networks of support (Kagan, 1992). Yet the social and political aspects of school are often the most important factors affecting teachers' decisions to continue teaching (Hollingsworth, Dybdahl, & Minarik, 1993; Ingersoll & Smith, 2004).

This chapter offers a framework for understanding new teacher support approaches and overviews research and theory on how support functions in social networks. My teacher support framework, the Continuum of New Teacher Support, synthesizes research on ideological perspectives on teacher professionalism into a classification of approaches to new teacher support. I demonstrate how to examine and characterize teacher support using the Continuum. Next, I explain how support is conceptualized within social network theory, and what researchers have found about the ways that networks can impact access to support.

TWO PERSPECTIVES ON NEW TEACHER SUPPORT

Studies on early career teachers have found that new teacher support through one-on-one mentoring, participation in professional communities, and induction can improve teacher retention and quality—*if* these activities share a particular set of characteristics. The Continuum of Teacher Support helps to identify whether a support person or program demonstrates these characteristics. It is called a continuum because a person or program does not usually fall neatly into one category. The continuum framework can help teachers develop a sense of who to reach out to or what kinds of support programs may help them. If teachers feel as if they are having trouble locating support, it may help them to re-evaluate their support network and seek individuals or groups that meet more of the framework criteria for high-quality teacher support.

Notions of support in this framework are rooted in ideologies about teaching and schooling. One perspective argues that teachers' work is social work, their praxis evolves through their interactions with colleagues, and that teacher agency should be valued. In this book, I call this ideological conceptualization of teaching the *Reform Perspective*. Alternatively, a more traditional view of teaching (which is still engrained in much of our thinking about schools and teachers) is that the teacher works in isolation on an assigned, inflexible curriculum. As such, I call this view the *Traditional Perspective*. The Reform and Traditional Perspectives represent two ends of the continuum.

The Continuum framework allows us to delve beyond the surface description of a support practice to see to what extent it reflects Reform or Traditional Perspectives on teacher support. Support practices can be evaluated as to where they exist on the continuum based on five key factors: time span of support, influence on the norms of teaching, degree of interactions with others in the school community, the occupational definition of "teacher," and teacher agency with the curriculum. Research on teacher support has demonstrated that high-quality support generally reflects characteristics of the Reform Perspective factors (Darling-Hammond & McLaughlin, 1995; Feiman-Nemser, Schwille, Carver, & Yusko, 1999; Lieberman, 1995; Little, 2001).

The New Teacher Support Continuum

Table 2.1 shows the five factors of the Continuum of New Teacher Support and the characteristics of support for the two ends of the Continuum. The first factor, Norms of Teaching, relates most closely to the core elements of each perspective. Support practices that encourage authentic collegiality (not forced or weak, as in "contrived collegiality" [Little, 1990]), sharing ideas, and leadership development among teachers reflect the Reform Perspective. Conversely, practices that encourage individual work, privacy, and equal status (no potential for leadership) reflect the Traditional Perspective. The second factor, professional interaction, relates closely with the first factor. This factor considers how teachers are encouraged to interact with each other—encouragement to work on their own reflects the Traditional Perspective and encouragement to work with others and collaborate supports the Reform Perspective.

Table 2.1. The Continuum of New Teacher Support

Factors	Traditional Perspective	Reform Perspective
Norms of teaching	Privacy, individual, isolation, equal status	Collegiality, openness, trust, leadership
Professional interaction	Isolated	Collaborative
Time span	Short term, infrequent (less than once a month)	Long term, frequent (more than once a month)
Occupational definition	Technician	Professional
Curriculum agency	Reproduction/delivery	Reflective/constructive/critique

Time Span of a support practice, the third factor, is also related to the first factor—when teachers meet frequently and over the long term, they are more likely to collaborate and develop trust. Thus, frequent, long-term interactions support the ability to collaborate and therefore reflect the Reform Perspective. When teachers meet for one-shot workshops, or less than once a month, the underlying assumption is that the workshop is meant for the individual to develop his or her practice in isolation, rather than through collaboration. Short-term and infrequent support is a sign of the Traditional Perspective.

Another sign of the Traditional Perspective is when teachers' jobs are considered that of technicians—their knowledge of teaching has no relevance to the broader knowledge base on teaching, their administrators make choices for them, and they enact those decisions. This represents the fourth factor—the Occupational Definition that is the subtext of the support practice. The Reform Perspective considers teachers to be professionals—making decisions based on their knowledge and experience, and contributing to our knowledge base on teaching. The final factor, Curriculum Agency, deals specifically with curricula on this issue—Reform Perspective practices support teacher agency, the evolution of a curricula, and the ability of the teacher to critique and change curricula to suit the students' needs. Traditional Perspective practices suggest that teachers deliver curricula as is—or as they are told.

From this review of factors, the Reform and Traditional Perspectives seem quite distinct from each other. However, in reality, most support practices (in programs and support from individuals) are a blend of these factors. The Continuum can help reveal the nature of support practices and their potential to retain quality teachers, as demonstrated in the following example analysis.

An Example Analyzing of New Teacher Support

This example is a description of the professional development training that Susan (a first-year teacher described more fully in Chapter 6) received at her school. Initially, Susan enjoyed the trainings, especially because she got to know the principal. However, over time she felt disillusioned about the trainings and did not see them as helpful, but rather, a burden.

> Susan attended a professional development program at her school once a month. The principal ran the training. The district often dictated the topics, yet at times the principal was able to customize it or add additional information that was pertinent to the teachers. The topics focused on the use of the mandated curriculum, the implementation of assessments, and examination of test scores. Teachers did not have a choice in the topic and were restricted in their talk about their practice to the topic at hand. The principal brought curriculum company trainers in from time to time to speak with the teachers, but the teachers did not present topics.

The following is a sample analysis of the program.

Factor 1: Norms of teaching. The Traditional Perspective's norms of teaching include isolationism and a passive role in curriculum development. Reform Perspective norms of teaching embrace teacher collaboration and voice. In Susan's program, the teachers were rarely offered the opportunity to voice their concerns and needs; rather, the information was given to them to accept and implement. Further, the facilitator controlled the dialogue so the teachers were not given the opportunity to collaborate with each other. For this factor, then, the program reflects the Traditional end of the Continuum.

Factor 2: Professional interactions. Some school districts amass their teachers at one location and then group teachers randomly for professional development. Susan's trainings were held at her school, which gave teachers the opportunity to focus on their school community. This aspect of the program reflects the Reform Perspective, because it demonstrates that the leaders value unique perspectives and relationships developed by the teacher community.

Factor 3: Time span. Although teachers met over the course of the year, they met only once a month, the bare minimum to be considered frequent support. Therefore, on the first factor, the induction workshop more closely aligns with the Traditional Perspective. If teachers met more frequently, the program would have been more indicative of the Reform Perspective, because teachers would have had a greater chance to collaborate and build relationships with others through the program.

Factor 4: Role of the teacher. Teachers in the program were instructed on the mandated curriculum and policies in an isolated manner, with little room for discussion about their own challenges. This reflects the perspective that administrators should control teachers' decisions, rather than allow them to make informed decisions (a Reform-end Perspective). Thus, this factor fits with the Traditional end of the Continuum.

Factor 5: Teacher's relationship with the curriculum. Did the program encourage teachers to develop the curriculum to fit the needs of their students and their teaching strengths? Or did it expect the teacher to implement an exact form of the curriculum? As with most of the other factors, the program clearly reflects a Traditional Perspective on curriculum by keeping a strict focus on the mandated curriculum throughout the workshops. Alternatively, the induction program could have supported teachers in developing curricula and lesson plans that reflect their students' needs and interests.

CONCLUSION:
A (MOSTLY) TRADITIONAL PROGRAM

The professional development program in Susan's school resides on the Traditional side of the Continuum. Although on the surface it may have seemed that the school was addressing contemporary research on teacher support by providing ongoing workshops, on closer examination, the Continuum framework showed that the program was replicating Traditional practices of schooling and professional development (see Table 2.2). Susan's disillusioned response to the professional development workshops fits with the pattern of findings that suggests that new teachers tend to seek out support reflecting Reform Perspective factors (Anderson, 2010; McCormick et al., 2010; Tellez, 1992). If the principal had planned to provide a higher-quality professional development program (reflecting the Reform Perspective), one thing he or she could have done is to allow for teachers to present and share their own work.

In addition to examining programs, the Continuum can also be used to evaluate the kinds of support that formal mentors, administrators, or colleagues offer to teachers. As such, when we look closely at teacher networks, an important characteristic to examine is where a network member fits in the Continuum. New teachers' disinclination toward Traditional support helps to explain the successes of programs or support people that strongly reflect Reform Perspective factors. The Continuum therefore helps to reveal the types of support that new teachers may be offered—the next framework examines how social networks work in providing access to these supports.

Table 2.2. Analysis of Susan's In-Service Professional Development Program, Using the Continuum of New Teacher Support

Factors	Traditional Perspective	Reform Perspective
Norms of teaching	Individualism	
Professional interaction		Allows for collaboration
Time span	Less than once a month	Long term
Occupational definition	Technician	
Curriculum agency	Delivery	

SOCIAL NETWORKS AND SUPPORT

Scholars have learned that social networks are a source for emotional, social, and financial support for people and communities. In addition, individuals can be strategic in seeking people and groups that can best support their work. There is an old Russian proverb, *ne imey sto rubley, a imey sto druzey,* which roughly translates to: "It's better to have a hundred friends than to have a hundred dollars" (or rubles, if you're in Russia). This concept, that there is value in relationships, is the basis for social network theory. social capital is the term used to represent the value that exists in social networks. Researchers work to learn about how social capital develops, functions, and changes inside a social network.

The Social Capital of a Social Network

The notion of social capital first became popular around the 1960s, when economists began to look beyond the concept of financial capital and considered less visible forms of capital that people could acquire through experiences or relationships. Three of these new forms include: human capital, cultural capital, and social capital. Largely credited with generating these theories are: Pierre Bourdieu (cultural and social capital), Gary S. Becker (human capital), James Coleman (social capital), and Robert Putman (social capital) (Anheier, Gerhards, & Romo, 1995; Coleman, 1990; Lin, 1999; Musial, 1999; Putnam, 1995; Stone & Wehlage, 1994).

Scholars have suggested that social capital is unique from other forms of capital in three ways. First, social capital can be depleted if it is *not* used and increase when it is used—when a person seeks out support from another in their network, they may build a trust and rapport that can increase their access to resources in the future (Burt & Minor, 1983). Second, yet in the same line of thinking, unlike financial capital, social capital needs constant maintenance—if network members do not interact, their relationships (and

NETWORKING TIP

To read more stories of support-seeking and professional development shared by teachers, visit www.thenetworkedteacher.com/#!community

social capital) will weaken. And finally, some forms of social capital are considered "collective goods"—not contained in people, but in the relationships between people (Adler & Kwon, 2002), such as the norms and trust developed between members of a church (Coleman, 1987). These factors make social capital dynamic, ever shifting, and very difficult to measure.

Difficulties in Measuring Social Capital

Due to the dynamic and somewhat obscure nature of social capital, there is some controversy as to how to identify and measure social capital. Further, these differences have led to a split in viewpoints as to what characteristics of social networks are most effective in producing social capital. There are two general schools of thought concerning the nature of social capital. The first is a communal view of social capital. In this perspective, social capital exists within a community and cannot be measured on an individual basis. The second is an individual view of social capital; individuals can possess and develop social capital through their social networks. Some scholars have attempted to resolve these controversies by looking closely at the characteristics of social capital that exist in different types of networks.

The Communal View of Social Capital

Communal social capital scholars argue that social capital exists within communities, not with individuals, and it increases as individuals in a community build relationships with each other—the more people in the network that know each other, the more opportunity for support and social capital. Sociologist Peter Coleman (1987) has contributed to this perspective through his research on families and schools. Coleman and colleagues studied dropout rates in Catholic schools, public schools, and other private schools. He concluded that the communal social capital developed in Catholic school communities provided support to students and lessened the likelihood that they drop out, as compared to the other school communities.

Another scholar in the communal social capital camp is Robert Putman (1995). Putman's research has focused on citizen involvement in civic groups. He suggests that when more individuals participate in civic associations and organizations, their social capital increases, which contributes to the civic capacity and democracy of a nation.

The concept of communal social capital has been used to develop theories of action for a range of community organizing groups, global nonprofit organizations, civic associations, and businesses (Freire, Henderson, & Kuncoro, 2010; Isham, Kolodinsky, & Kimberly, 2004). An example of such activity is exemplified through the work of a large-scale consultancy firm, Orgnet.com, which specializes in providing social network analysis software and services to a range of corporate clients, including the Annie E. Casey Foundation, MacArthur Foundation, Barr Foundation, and the Centers for Disease Control (Krebs, 2010). Lelong (as cited in Patton, 2005, p. 2) notes that these types of tools are popular with businesses because they "identi[fy] the go-to experts and can help companies find the technical knowledge within their organization needed to develop a new drug, launch a new product and stay ahead of the competition." The growth of online social network software has also popularized the notion of the power of social networks.

Related to this perspective is the notion of closed networks. A closed network is a network in which many members are connected to each other; it is a dense, multiconnected network, often with shared values, norms, and trust. This concept is related to the communal view of social capital because theorists from this perspective argue that this type of network (dense, closely connected individuals) provides high levels of social capital. According to this view, a social network with fewer ties (relationships between individuals) and more distant relationships would offer less social capital.

The Individual View of Social Capital

Social capital has also been conceptualized as an individual asset by a range of scholars. Under this individual perspective, scholars argue that social capital can be measured by examining characteristics of relationships between individuals in a network. A quantities research approach that is based in this perspective is called Social Network Analysis (Haythornthwaite, 1996; Wasserman & Faust, 1994; Wellman, 1983). Whereas in the communal view, social capital is generally perceived as trust or norms, in the individual view, social capital is usually thought of as the resources and information available in social networks (Borgatti & Foster, 2003; Lin, 2001).

Another difference between the communal and individual views of social capital is the individual view proponents' (particularly Social Network Analysis scholars) contention that social capital increases in open networks—that is, when individuals in a network are diverse (do not share many norms), and are *not* overly connected to each other through relationships. In this view, these kinds of networks provide a diverse array of knowledge and ideas, which lead to innovation and higher levels of social capital. Granovetter (1985), an early supporter of this view, argues that "weak ties" (links with individuals that were not densely connected with others in a network or community) were valuable in networks.

Combining the Views

Scholars who take the communal view see social capital as a collective measure and generally value tight-knit (closed) networks, which can develop shared norms and values more easily. Social Network Analysis scholars and others who take the individual view believe that it is possible to measure an individual's social capital, and, through their research, have found benefits to loosely linked networks and ties (open networks). Although these two perspectives seem at odds, some scholars have attempted to find a middle ground between the two. Lin (1999) suggests that open and closed networks provided *different types* of social capital. Closed networks provide support and trust, while open networks lead to innovation and adaptation. This distinction supports the findings of both groups of scholars; if trust and support represent social capital, then it would increase through closed networks; however, if innovation and access to new resources represents social capital, then it would increase through open networks.

In this book, I use Lin's compromise view on social capital measures, yet I borrow from the individual view the idea that individuals can develop, gain, and have social capital. The aim here is to use a perspective that will help teachers see their own roles in social networks and network development—as agents of change that have some power in developing support networks. Thus, Lin's compromise allows me to ask: If different types of social capital are increased by two radically different structures of social networks, what kinds of networks build social capital and thus, support, for new teachers?

To answer this question requires an examination of teachers' social networks and spurs additional questions, for example, do network structures relate in any way to characteristics of teachers' support as framed by the Continuum? Also, what types of networks do new teachers tend to develop? As this chapter has established a basis for understanding characteristics of new teacher support and the functioning of support within social networks, it provides an avenue to explore these questions, and more. In Chapter 3, I describe what we know about support in new teachers' social networks and illustrate four cases of new teacher networks. From this examination arises a second framework, which identifies two types of social networks that have been found to provide professional support to new teachers: Intentional Professional Networks and Diverse Professional Allies.

CHAPTER 3

Looking at Networks:
Network Types and the Networking
Practices of New Teachers

Until the last 10 years or so, there was very little research on the social networks of teachers (Penuel & Riel, 2007). The history of research on teacher communities is longer; however, this field is also still developing. Although there is abundant research on schools as communities and on students' lives, in comparison teacher communities only became recognized as an important factor in shaping school life relatively recently (in the last 25 years). The research community's acknowledgment of the role of the teacher in shaping curriculum has pushed scholars to learn more about how teachers' relationships and interactions impact their work (Rowan, 1990).

This chapter serves to examine the existing research on teachers' social networks, describe frameworks for identifying types of teacher support networks, and illustrate these concepts through the examination of four new teachers' social support networks. One issue that will become evident throughout the chapter is the challenges that new teachers may face in seeking support through their networks. At times, the coping mechanisms that new teachers use to seek support can become counteractive. Thus, the teacher support network typology framework can offer some guidance to new teachers and their advocates toward creating robust networks of support.

WHAT WE KNOW ABOUT
SOCIAL NETWORKS AND TEACHING

The early scholars on teacher relationships searched for concepts that could focus on networks for knowledge exchange and learning communities. Lave and Wenger's (1991) concept of communities of practice theorizes that learning and knowledge are located within the relationships that make up a network and that people become acculturated into the communities of practice through a process of legitimate peripheral participation, in which they learn the norms and practice of the group.

However, the concept of the community of practice has recently been challenged due to its characterization of networks and communities of learning as stable and local (Brown & Duguid, 2001; Hakkarainen, Palonen, Paavola, & Lehtinen, 2004). Several theorists have developed alternative conceptions of networks that consider the dynamic and distributed nature of some knowledge-exchange networks: Knotworking and Intensional (*sic*) Networks. In Knotworking, a team of people pulls together for work on a specific project and disperses once the project is accomplished (Engestrom, Engestrom, & Vahaaho, 1999). Knotworking is dynamic, short-term, and often composed of people who may not know each other previously or have strong ties; they collaborate because of complementary skill sets.

Intensional Networks are egocentric, personal networks of people called on to accomplish a task or project (Nardi, Whittaker, & Schwartz, 2000, 2002). For example, if a businessperson wanted to promote his product, he might first call on people in his personal social network that he is familiar with and has done work with before prior to going outside this network. These personal contact "first responders" are the businessperson's Intensional Network. Intensional Networks were spelled "intensional" because the people in the networks are deliberately chosen, and there is *tension* in the great stress of managing these networks, but they also provide flexibility (*tensile* strength). Intensional Networks are becoming increasingly relevant because of the high degree of fluctuation in organizations, which leads people to rely more on personal networks.

More recently, social network research has been applied to educational contexts (Daly, 2010a). New ideas about knowledge sharing and networks have led to research on teachers' social networks. Studies on teacher networks have revealed how informal networks shape a range of school outcomes from academic achievement to curriculum implementation and teacher turnover. social networks shape teachers' choices about where they work, and whether they stay at their jobs. They mediate their interpretations of new policies or curricula and determine their access to new information about teaching and reforms. Social networks influence teachers' professional identities and their socialization and leadership abilities at schools. Finally, social networks impact teachers' professional development and their ability to support student achievement. Table 3.1 shows a list of recent findings and research topics on teachers' social networks. The findings and theories show the important role of social networks in teachers' lives and contribute to the framework for understanding teachers' social networks presented in this book.

Table 3.1. Recent Scholarship on Teachers' Social Networks

Feature	Findings	Studies
Commitment and turnover	Teachers with social support networks that are based primarily at their own school are more likely to stay. However, if these teachers leave, they are also more likely to catalyze others to leave.	(Baker-Doyle, 2010; Thomas, 2007)
Work location	Teachers tend to apply for jobs in places where their social networks have structural similarity to home networks.	(Boyd, Lankford, Loeb, & Wycoff, 2003)
Innovation and curriculum development	Teachers with diverse networks tend to have more innovative curriculum. Also, social networks affect teachers' implementation of innovative curricula just as much as their training or access to resources.	(Baker-Doyle, in press; Frank et al., 2004)
Implementation of curriculum	Teachers' use of curriculum is shaped by their social interactions, i.e., teachers who collaborate or interact with others are better able to cope with change.	(Bidwell & Yasumoto, 1999; Coburn, 2001; Lieberman, 2000)
Leadership	School leaders are central figures in school social networks. Leadership is shaped by the social networks in a school.	(Daly et al., 2009; Spillane et al., 2004)
School reform	The way teachers and administrators develop advice networks and friendship networks impacts the outcomes of school reform.	(Daly et al., 2009; Daly, 2010b; McCormick et al., 2010; Moolenaar, 2010)

Socialization and community support	Networks can impact how teachers locate support and help them learn to navigate the politics of their school.	(Anderson, 2010; Baker-Doyle, in press; Lieberman & Miller, 1999; Spillane, 1999; Thomas, 2007b)
Professional development	Characteristics of a school or program's approach to professional development can shape teachers' networks in ways that help or harm the outcomes of the program.	(Baker-Doyle & Yoon, 2010; Penuel et al., 2009)
Teacher knowledge and expertise	When teachers are made aware of the content expertise and teaching experiences of others in their networks or community, advice networks evolve and can spur collaboration.	(Baker-Doyle & Yoon, 2010; Coburn, Choi, & Mata, 2010)
Self-efficacy and teacher identity	Teachers with strong Intentional Professional Networks more easily develop a sense of teacher identity and self efficacy.	(Baker-Doyle, in press)
Academic outcomes	Teachers with strong support networks have a greater likelihood of success with implementing new curricula and fostering student achievement.	(Boyd, Grossman, Lankford, Loeb, & Wycoff, 2006; Spillane, 2000; Spillane & Thompson, 1997; Yasumoto, Uekawa, & Bidwell, 2001)

A FRAMEWORK FOR UNDERSTANDING
TEACHERS' SOCIAL NETWORKS

The Continuum of Professional Support described in Chapter 2 identified characteristics of high-quality support for new teachers. The most intense Reform-end support for new teachers tends to come from professional colleagues who work collaboratively in the same school context, on an informal basis. These localized collaborative professional relationships form what I call teachers' *Intentional Professional Networks* (Baker-Doyle, in press). An Intentional Professional Network is a teacher's network of the people they select to collaborate and interact with to solve professional problems. Intentional Professional Networks are local (most often, in the school), professional relationships, formed through active problem solving, that result in strong ties between the teachers and their Intentional Professional Network contacts. Intentional Professional Network contacts help new teachers to navigate the norms of their schools, establish their status and professional identity, solve everyday problems, and feel more confident about their work. In contrast to a teachers' professional community of practice, Intentional Professional Networks are viewed from the standpoint of the individual and the compositions of the networks are dynamic; they depend on the immediate project or problem.

While the most intense Reform-end support comes from Intentional Professional Networks, another influential form of support can be found through individuals who are not frequently recognized as support persons by new teachers: *Diverse Professional Allies*. Diverse Professional Allies are nontraditional support providers who are not usually considered "professionals," such as parents, volunteers, or students. Diverse Professional Allies are invested in the professional growth of the teachers. They help teachers challenge the traditional norms of the school or teaching and break out of notions about curriculum or practice that limited the teachers' personal involvement in the curriculum.

As diverse, atypical, more distant relationships, Diverse Professional Allies are what network researchers call "boundary-crossing ties." Boundary-crossing ties have been found to bring in new, innovative information that is important to challenging information redundancy in networks (Cross et al., 2003; Gallucci, 2003; Hakkarainen et al., 2004). Boundary crossing is difficult work; it requires people to challenge their assumptions and reach out to others that they may not know how to interact with. People tend to gravitate toward people of similar professional backgrounds, status, and race (Hinds, Carley, Krackhardt, & Wholey, 2000). Further, in dynamic networks teachers need to develop these relationships quickly, across many contexts. With all their difficulty, however, boundary-crossing ties can provide important resources and support (Hakkarainen et al., 2004). In schools, specifically, strong ties with parents and community members have been shown to increase a teacher's interest in and likelihood of remaining at a school (Hargreaves, 2000; Johnson & Birkeland, 2003; Montano & Burstein, 2006). Although parents and community members are historically perceived as teachers' adversaries, they can provide a range of support in partnership with teachers (Carmichael, Fox, McCormick, Proctor, & Honour, 2006; Lawrence-Lightfoot, 2003; Strieb, 2010).

This framework addresses one of the primary debates in Social Network Theory literature: What networks are most beneficial in terms of social capital—open networks with weak ties or closed networks with strong ties? For the cases of these teachers, the answer is, both. Intentional Professional Networks are close, often closed, networks that provide access, stability, and some new ideas to the teachers. Diverse Professional Allies are diverse, disconnected to many others in the network, and have weaker ties. Diverse Professional Allies spur innovation, challenge traditional norms, and work behind the scenes.

When new teachers recognize the role of social support networks in their work, they may realize that they are not as alone as they thought they were, they may challenge themselves to build bridges with other teachers or parents, or they may make conscious, strategic decisions to collaborate with others. Then, on the first day of school, they might be armed with more than pedagogical and content knowledge—they might be armed with the power of social networks.

THE REALITY OF NEW TEACHER NETWORKS

The framework for understanding teachers' social support networks I've described highlights two types of networks that provide invaluable support to new teachers. In reality, there is a wide range of networks and relationships that new teachers rely on for support during their early years. Some of these networks offer weak or inappropriate types of support for the teachers. In the following section, I describe four different networks, which represent a range of support networks that new teachers may have. Of the examples, one of these networks is highly effective at providing support for new teachers and reflects the frameworks described earlier; two of the networks represent very typical new teacher networks, and is a network with insufficient access to valuable resources and support.

New teacher networks are different from networks of experienced teachers in several ways. First, the new teacher is likely entering a school with little or no relationships to others in the school. Therefore, initially, a new teacher's network is highly dependent on outsiders for support. Second, new teachers seek out different forms of support than experienced teachers.

New teachers need to learn how to socialize and understand the politics of the school, as well as work on developing a teacher identity. Third, so-called millennial (Safer, 2007) teachers, Americans born after 1980, tend to develop and use networks in different ways than the earlier generations. The millennial generation's job seeking and career development practices are dynamic and depend strongly on networking outside of their workplaces. I conclude this chapter with a review of the generational factors that make today's new teacher networks unique, and explain how they can impact new teachers' experiences and network development.

Looking at the Social Networks of New Teachers: Four Cases

In Chapter 2, I discussed two views of social capital—the communal view and the individual view. To examine the dynamics of a new teachers' network, I take an individual view of social capital from an egocentric perspective. This means that I describe the network as it relates to one person (the new teacher), rather than the network as a whole (for example, all teachers at one school or across several schools). This perspective allows me to show the trends and characteristics of the people to whom new teachers reach out to for support; it is centered on the new teachers' experiences in locating support.

With this individualist perspective come certain methods of measuring and comparing networks. One measure is network density. Density is the degree to which people in one network are linked to each other. In mathematical terms, the density of a network is the number of network ties divided by the number of all possible ties. If a network is very dense, many people in the network have ties to each other. If it is not dense, only ties are sparse in a network.

Another important issue to consider in an egocentric network is size. Size can dictate density in some ways—larger networks are likely less dense than smaller networks. Size can also show whether the person at the center of an egocentric network may be too stressed (too many ties), or, conversely, isolated (very few ties in certain contexts, such as a workplace).

Finally, the attributes of individuals in a network can reveal information about the strength of a relationship, trends in network members' demographics, and patterns of interaction between network members. In looking at support networks of teachers, we can consider where support lives or works, the kind of support they provide, type of relationship (professional, friend, administrator, etc.), years of teaching experience, and a number of other teacher support-related characteristics. Attributes, network size, and density are the measures I use in describing the following four teacher network examples.

No two networks are alike, and no network is static. Yet, snapshots of networks can be helpful to examine for access to the different forms of support and the support network types (Intentional Professional Networks and

Diverse Professional Allies) discussed in Chapter 2. In Chapters 5 and 6, I tell the stories of Maria, Susan, Steven, and Michael's first years. Here, their networks are used as examples of the range of new teacher support networks. These networks represent the most influential members of the teachers' support networks. The first example describes Maria's network, which is highly effective at accessing reform support—very rare for a new teacher. The second and third examples are Susan and Steven's networks, respectively. Their networks represent typical new teacher networks, both with unique circumstances and characteristics. Finally, Michael's network shows inadequate access to support, yet is not atypical for a new teacher network.

With each example, a network diagram is provided to illustrate the teachers' support network. The diagram shows the people sought by teachers for teaching support during their first year. They represent self-reported and observed ties. In other words, they include the support persons recalled by the teachers and the individuals who were observed to provide teaching support in school. The following key to the network diagrams explains the ties and characteristics of individuals in the teachers' networks.

KEY FOR FIGURES 3.1—3.5:

Each shape is an influential person in the teachers' social support network. The shape and color indicate their role and location.

Shapes:

- Circle: Focus teacher
- Octagon: In Intentional Professional Network
- Diamond: In Diverse Professional Ally Network
- Triangle: Offers limited or traditional support

Colors:

- Gray: Works in Focus teachers' school
- White: Works outside of teachers' school

Example 1: Maria. Maria's network shows a large Intentional Professional Network (six) and a fair number of Diverse Professional Allies (two) (see Figure 3.1). These network types foster strong Reform support. Her Intentional Professional Network existed inside and outside of her school—yet those outside of her school came to visit her frequently and had a strong knowledge of the context and content of her teaching. In some cases, her personal ties overlapped with her professional ties, providing greater acces-

Figure 3.1. Maria's Social Support Network

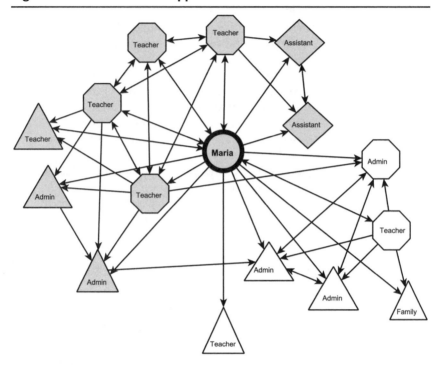

sibility and information exchange throughout the network. You will read in the next few chapters about how and why Maria's network was somewhat unusual in its large Intentional Professional Network and the robust support that network members provided.

Example 2: Susan. Susan's network shows a small Intentional Professional Network (three), and a larger group of colleagues outside school (see Figure 3.2). Many of these colleagues were friends from her teacher education programs; like her, they were first-year teachers. The size and density of this out-of-school subgroup was very high. Susan's network is typical for first-year teachers in that many of her support members were outside the school, and were unable to provide professional support, mainly due to infrequent contact or a weak knowledge of her teaching context. Susan struggled throughout the year to develop more relationships in school. Ultimately, she developed relationships with many Diverse Professional Allies, who provided valuable insight and motivation for her practice. You can also see in this map how one teacher was a link between the Diverse Professional Allies and Susan's other school colleagues. In Chapter 6, you will read more about how this teacher acted as a bridge for Susan to develop her Diverse Professional Ally network.

Figure 3.2. Susan's Social Support Network

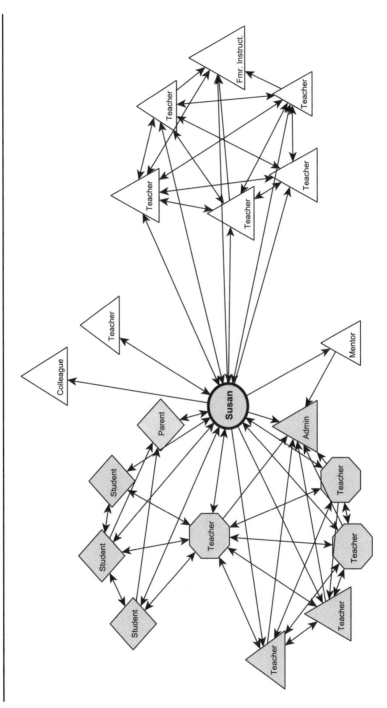

Figure 3.3. Steven's Social Support Network

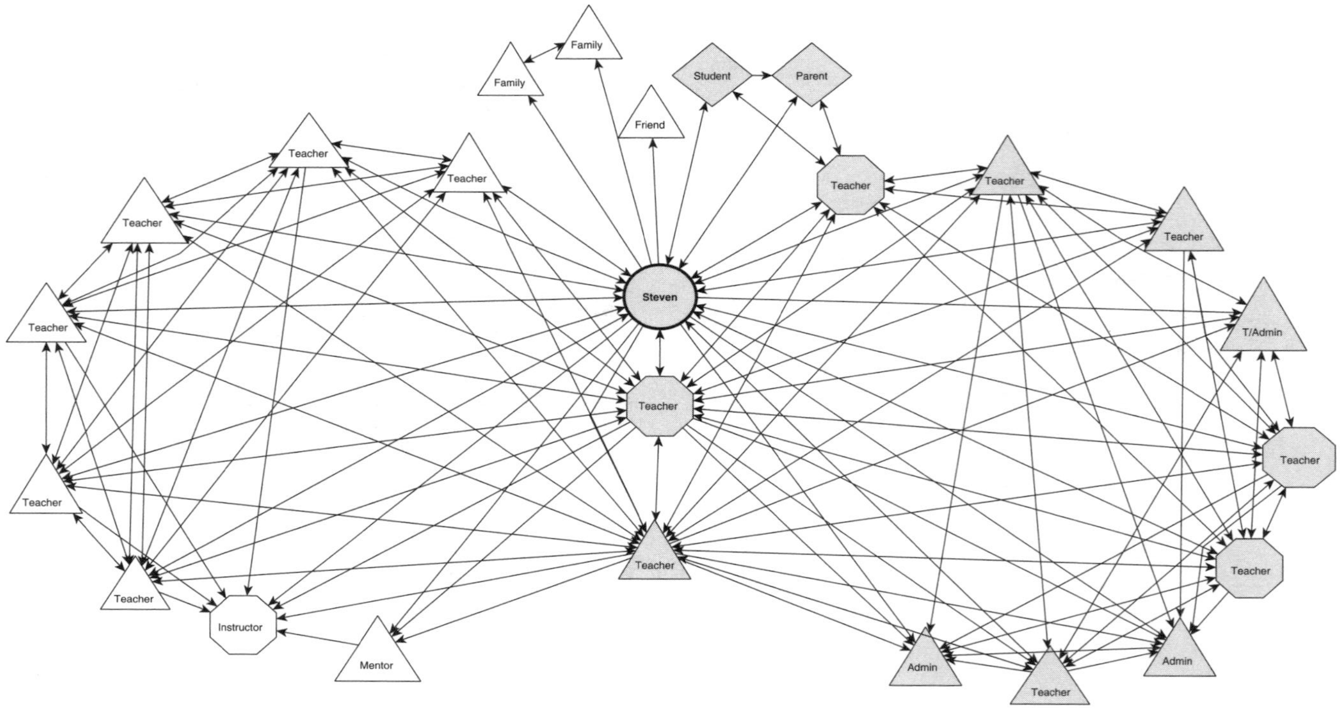

Example 3: Steven. Like Susan, Steven's network is typical for new teachers—a balance of support from inside and outside the school (see Figure 3.3). Although his network is the largest network presented here, he had a relatively small Intentional Professional Network at his school (four colleagues). This was because many of the colleagues at his school offered Traditional support, which was frustrating for Steven; he noted often that he did not find this support useful. Also similar to Susan, Steven's contacts outside of school were mainly first-year teachers, whom he found to provide strong emotional support but not intense professional support.

Example 4: Michael. Michael had a small network of primarily family and friends outside his school (see Figure 3.4). Described in detail in Chapter 5, Michael's struggles as a first-year teacher were strongly related to his small Intentional Professional Network. However, his story, like his network, is common for first-year teachers.

Figure 3.4. Michael's Social Support Network

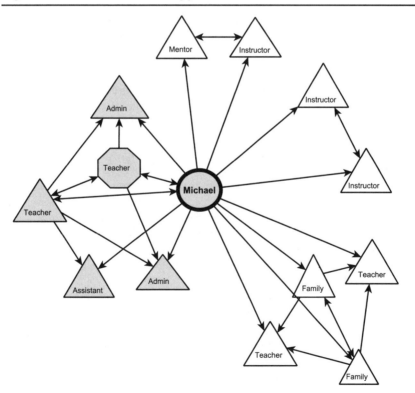

New teacher networks generally have more out-of-school support from family and friends than support from Intentional Professional Networks and Diverse Professional Ally networks, exemplified by Susan's network diagram. Sometimes they do not receive effective support from colleagues at their schools due to the school culture and atmosphere, which emphasize traditional support, as seen in Steven's case (this is discussed further in Chapter 4). Further, they often do not acknowledge the support they receive from Diverse Professional Allies. Some of these trends can be explained by teachers' lack of understanding of networking for support, and they can also be explained by the first-year experience and generational differences, which I discuss next.

COMMUNICATION AND COLLABORATION PRACTICES OF THE MILLENNIAL GENERATION

The notion of a millennial generation is contested—generalizing the attitudes and practices of an entire generation is certainly problematic. However, the children who grew up during the 1990s and 2000 were faced with unique circumstances not endured by any previous generation. First, economically, job stability disappeared—people moved from job to job more frequently as technology replaced many lifelong middle-class jobs. Second, these individuals experienced 9/11 through children's eyes, and the ensuing wars in Iraq and Afghanistan have been a constant since then. Third, schooling and parenting methods have changed: These are the children of NCLB, but also the kids whose textbooks represented a wide range of ethnicities and perspectives. They are the children who all received a trophy at the end of a game, whether or not they won. Yet it is perhaps the changes in the way we communicate that have had the most significant impact on this generation. With the advent of the Internet, smart phones, laptops, and portable multimedia devices, our notion of staying in touch has changed forever—and for the millennials, it has forever been a part of their lives. With these shared experiences, we can identify some shared patterns of interaction and networking behavior, which also, not surprisingly, reflect the teacher turnover problems that U.S. schools have experienced since the early 1990s.

The first trend is seen in the network diagrams shown previously; millennials develop strong networks outside of their workplace—and maintain these relationships over the long term. This practice makes sense considering the job market—because careers rarely last a lifetime at one job, it is necessary to develop a broader network in case one needs to locate a new job. However, millennials have taken a step ahead of this situation—instead of waiting for a job to disappear, many millennials have no problem with the idea of moving from one job to another, and will take the initiative to do

> ## NETWORKING TIP
>
> *To make your own support network map with our online network mapping tool, or to see more examples of other teachers' support networks, visit www.thenetworkedteacher.com/#!resources*

it themselves if not satisfied at their own jobs. For new teachers, this relates strongly to teacher turnover; teachers who don't develop strong Intentional Professional Networks at their schools (instead relying more on outside support), become unhappy, and leave for another job.

Technology also plays a big role in the turnover trend. millennials are able to maintain long-term relationships outside their workplace through technology. They are used to constant interaction with their peers, which can avert their efforts to develop face-to-face relationships at work. The perception that "help is out there"—somewhere on Wikipedia or a Google search—can dissuade new teachers from seeking support in their own backyards. To reduce teacher turnover, one challenge we have is to optimize the use of technology for networking and support—which means focusing on building networks in the workplace instead of other locations through cyberspace.

The notion of searching for information has changed with the Internet. In the same way, for millennials, the concept of a boss or leader has changed. millennials expect their leaders to be like coaches—guiding them, cheering them on, without overemphasis on authority. The idea of a coach and a team resonates strongly with millennials, who grew up with cooperative learning and an emphasis on fairness and justice. When seeking support at a school, new Millennial teachers would probably avoid dogmatic authority figures, and instead look for coach-like leaders who take a teambuilding approach. School leaders can use this as an advantage to support teacher networking by working collaboratively with new teachers and fostering professional teamwork.

Another aspect of the millennial generation that can be useful in supporting network development is the millennial perspective on diversity. Due to more multicultural curricula and more opportunities to see and work with people of different backgrounds (as a result of increased access to technology, media, and transportation), millennials had more exposure to diversity than previous generations. Their exposure to such diversity may help them to be more open to the idea of collaborating with parents and community members to develop Diverse Professional Allies. School leaders have a role to play in setting the stage for this behavior, through providing examples and opportunities for community involvement.

THE MILLENNIAL NETWORKER

Millennial teachers embody many characteristics that can help them develop an effective support network. They have vast experience and knowledge in communicating through technology, they are attuned to notions of teamwork and collaboration, and many have been exposed to diverse cultures and practices. Yet, without a strong understanding of how to strategically develop networks for support, many will use their networking advantage to seek employment in another career if they are unsatisfied with teaching. In this chapter, I have shared some examples of what teacher networks can look like. In the following chapters, you will read about what shaped these networks, and how the networks impacted teachers' experiences. These stories share lessons in themselves; in the final chapter, I describe strategies that teachers can use to be conscious networkers—to use the advantages of being millennial teachers in developing effective support networks.

CHAPTER 4

Inside Schools:
School Culture Shaping
Teachers' Networks

New teachers are not the only ones that can actively develop effective social support networks—the culture and organization of a school also shape teachers' social networks (Kardos, Johnson, Peske, Kauffman, & Liu, 2001; Saronson, 1971; Weiss, 1999). The number of meetings or mentoring programs in a school is not the sole factor that influences teachers' networking. Although an important part of supporting teachers' collaboration is to offer them opportunities to meet and time for planning, time means very little if the school culture is focused only on test score outcomes rather than supporting teacher inquiry and the *process* of learning to teach.

New teachers have many questions. Their questions arise from their daily work with students, faculty, and administration. Often these questions are related to their personal beliefs and experiences, and are specific to a classroom or a student. Teachers in test-focused schools spend their time in meetings answering other people's questions and not their own. Effective social support networks develop through active collaboration on teachers' own problems. When teachers are discouraged from seeking out the answers to their own questions, they are also discouraged from seeking out collaborators and informal mentors.

In this chapter you will read about three very different urban middle schools and new teachers in these schools. The stories illustrate the impact of an outcomes-based school culture on teacher networking and collaboration. Each approached teachers' support and development in distinctive ways: Northpoint school took a laissez faire approach to teacher support, Bailey school reflected a balanced approach, and Bernard school was aggressively top down in training and supporting teachers. However, despite the diversity in approaches, each school culture was test focused, and thus the new teachers in the schools faced steep challenges in locating support and developing their support networks.

NORTHPOINT MIDDLE SCHOOL: LAISSEZ FAIRE

Michael and Maria were both teachers at Northpoint High School, a small neighborhood school serving 8th-, 9th-, and 10th-graders. There were about 360 students in the school, and 24 staff and faculty members. In 2005, 97% of the students were African American, and 88% of the students qualified for free lunch (NCES). Northpoint was considered a high school in transition; previously a middle school, it was being converted, year by year, into a high school. True to its categorization, everything about the school was in transition. The principal and vice principal were new to the school, as were 10 out of the 16 faculty members. Further, the 10 new teachers were not only new to the school but new to the career as well. The school was being managed by an outside, nonprofit contractor, which provided additional resources in the form of materials, professional development, and additional staff. In July 2007, the school closed under mysterious circumstances; though media reports suggested that the school closed due to building problems, the most recent maintenance report for the school listed no violations, and teachers were told that the school closed due to low test scores.

What made the school feel the most transitional, was that there were no extracurricular activities available for students at the school for most of the year. Michael felt that he had less leverage with the students because he could not engage his students through interest in their activities. Maria felt that she was not able to get to know her students as well because she didn't have the opportunity to get to know them in a nonacademic setting. Overall, the lack of extracurricular opportunities engendered a feeling that the school lacked a soul; it was hard to get to know the culture of the school beyond exaggerated student antics and major crises. The lack of connection between the school and the students or the surrounding community made it difficult for the teachers to build relationships and networks within these communities. Michael and Maria did not begin to significantly reach out to parents or students until late in the spring.

At Northpoint, teachers were provided few organized opportunities to work with or meet colleagues. Maria and Michael would note with some depreciating humor that "teacher support" was a "foreign word" in the school, based on the administration's lack of constructive feedback or attention to teachers' planning needs. Classroom schedules did not overlap to provide joint planning time for grade or subject groups, and professional development meetings were developed with set agendas that did not allow for much collaboration between teachers. A district evaluation of contact providers done in 2007 reinforced these findings; they found that in schools run by the nonprofit, "the professional development is scripted and focused on data analysis and benchmarks."

Michael and Maria had emotional reactions to the school's laissez faire approach to teacher support. Maria was frustrated that she had to find times before or after school to talk with fellow teachers—it was an extra burden to her already busy schedule. Michael was not only frustrated—he felt disempowered by a loneliness fostered by the lack of support structures and pondered whether it was intentionally isolating, noting that, "in some ways I almost feel like they want to . . . keep us isolated, that makes us less powerful."

In addition to their struggles in finding time for collaboration, Michael and Maria had difficulty locating formal support from experienced mentors or administrators. The new teachers had not been initially assigned a teacher coach from the school district because, as it had been explained to them, the school had not reached Annual Yearly Progress (the baseline test score improvements necessary for receiving additional federal government funds) the year before. The nonprofit company that ran the school hired a coach in December to support the teachers; however, as Maria describes below, he became quickly ineffectual and rarely visited the teachers or offered any support.

> He's one of the people that I avoid . . . because I feel like he's gone over to the dark side. . . . He's trying to take a more administrative role. He's so negative. He actually tells people, "Look for a new job next year."

Yet, Maria and Michael interpreted the professional community and collegiality differently at the school. Michael felt that the lack of professional support structures forced a sense of isolationism among the teachers, noting:

> You can go through, almost the entire day . . . [and] feel like you've not interacted with a person. . . . Everybody's on their own—everybody's got their own domain, and they stick to it.

Conversely, Maria sensed potential camaraderie among the faculty as a defensive response to the perceived lack of concern by the administration. She felt she had to work hard to reach out, but that the outcomes of her efforts were positive. However, both Maria and Michael noted that the staff and faculty were disillusioned and saddened by the lack of formal or structured support in the schools. The differences in opinion between the two teachers on this topic, stemming from different experiences, networking behaviors, and interactions with network members, will be discussed in detail in Chapter 5.

BAILEY ELEMENTARY SCHOOL: TRADITIONAL MANAGEMENT

By formal measures, Bailey elementary offered more opportunities for professional collaboration and interaction and had higher standardized test scores than Northpoint. However, the focus on maintaining Annual Yearly Progress and raising test scores made the school environment stressful for many teachers, and there was an underlying sense of professional isolationism, perhaps from this stress, throughout most of the school. The social atmosphere between the teachers reflected this culture; teachers were expected to adhere strictly to a social code that dissuaded teachers from professional collaboration and inquiry. In reaction to this environment, Susan worked professionally with only the few teachers with whom she shared a common philosophy on teaching and working with students. While Susan's school may have differed from Northpoint by formal measures, the underlying orientation was the same; the professional culture of the school did not embrace teacher inquiry or professional conversations around curriculum and students needs, beyond raising test scores.

Bailey Elementary is a small, tight-knit elementary and middle school (kindergarten through 6th grade), with about 160 students, and one class per grade. About 93% of students at Bailey were African American, and almost 5% were Latino in 2006. In the school population, about 85% of the students were eligible for free or reduced lunch. Test scores in the school were higher than Philadelphia averages but lower than most state averages. Bailey had reached Annual Yearly Progress for the past 3 years, and it was evident from the signs and displays that this accomplishment brought both pride and increased pressure to the school. Like Northpoint, Bailey was managed by a nonprofit company hired by the school district to oversee the school.

The principal developed a number of structures and practices at Bailey to foster professional support for teachers. She allowed Susan to shadow two teachers for 3 days before beginning to teach at the school. She developed unique, in-house professional developments for the teachers, which were engaging and informing. Teachers and administrators jointly designed policies surrounding discipline, test-taking, and academic activities. Teachers were encouraged to socialize or meet with each other during their lunch period. Besides these structures, implemented primarily by the principal, Susan was also assigned a teacher coach from the school district mentoring program for about 3 months of the year (before the program was discontinued).

Although these programs and structures provided meeting time and professional support, Susan felt that they were not enough; she did not feel that the teachers supported each other professionally—the "culture" of professional support was weak. Instead, she sensed that teachers at Bailey were overwhelmed by the pressures to raise test scores and grade averages, and either were not interested or did not have the time to help each other.

Susan and her colleagues were frequently shown test data and student grades at their professional development meetings to problem solve and develop plans to increase scores. However, this also created increased pressure and blame among the teachers. Here, Susan describes this environment:

> I do feel partially [pressured] in a sense . . . because everybody knows everybody's business because the school's so small . . . if the 4th-grade test scores are not good it's my fault, if the 5th-grade test scores are not good, it's that teacher's fault, you know? . . . Some other teachers have their kids throwing up because of the [statewide standardized tests], like literally throwing up because they're so scared of it.

Susan also felt that the small size and intense focus on outcomes made it difficult for her to socialize and find help. During her first few days at the school, she was eager to work with others and asked for help from several teachers. Many teachers saw her inquiry-oriented stance as a bad mark on her ability to teach. Further, they felt intimidated when she asked to observe them because they worried about what she might say about them. There was an atmosphere of paranoia in the small school. Teachers didn't want to be burdened with others' questions—they were worried about themselves. Here Susan describes how she became aware of the school politics:

> I found out that—it's kind of like, every person for themselves . . . that was my first big lesson in the socialization of my school; learning the politics and knowing that you kind of have to do things on your own and just make sure what you tell people. Because . . . everything gets back to everyone else.

Susan spent a lot of her energy navigating through what she called a "field of landmines" created by the informal social structure, which ran somewhat counter to the formal structures. By the end of the year, she felt "let down" because she had to devote so much energy to this part of her job. She consciously spent time with other teachers who were *not* helpful to her professionally, but only for social survival in the school.

The underlying social "rules" of the school may have not been entirely known of or recognized by the administration. Susan was shocked that her principal expressed surprise when she learned that the school counselor rated the support environment of the school "poor" on an end-of-year district survey. This counselor was one of the few people who actively offered help to Susan in her first few days on the job.

Susan noted that she felt that the principal did support her on a personal level, through one-on-one meetings. The principal also conveyed her
support of Susan through positive praise not only in personal discussions
but also in announcements at staff meetings. However, her praise and personal interactions did not alter the general sense of exclusion that Susan felt
from the faculty.

BERNARD MIDDLE SCHOOL: TOP DOWN MANAGEMENT

Bernard Middle School made social codes in the school explicit, rather than
like the implicit social codes at Bailey. Students and teachers were constantly
reminded of the high expectations held for them on tests via motivational
posters, school sayings, promotional items, and rally-type events. The school
offered the greatest amount of professional development and collaboration
opportunities of all the example schools, and was the most unified in terms
of approach to discipline, curriculum, and school culture, which focused on
preparing students for the benchmark tests they took monthly, as well as the
statewide standardized tests. The explicit nature of the school culture made
it easy for Steven to participate in and join; however, as he developed his
professional practice, he began to question facets of the culture that made
it difficult to relate or respond to his students and meet his own needs. His
growing conceptualizations of pedagogy placed him at odds with the formal
supports and professional development opportunities in the school. Thus, as
did Michael, Maria, and Susan, he relied more on informal relationships for
professional support rather than the formal entities at the school because of
the intense focus on testing. One exception in Steven's case was that he did
greatly value the co-teaching opportunities within the school structure; the
co-teacher and his interests and needs, rather than the test-prep ideology of
the school, guided these opportunities.

Bernard Middle School is a mid-sized neighborhood school comprised
of about 600 7th- and 8th-graders. About 98% of the students attending
Bernard in 2006–7 were African American, and 84.6% were eligible for
free or reduced lunch (Urban School District, 2007). Bernard had a high
rate of student mobility; over the course of the 2006 school year, 200 new
students entered mid-year, and 148 withdrew, which was close to half of the
student population. The school test scores were slightly below district averages, despite a strong focus on the testing in the school.

Bernard was a public school managed by a private company. The company was known for its unique literacy and mathematics curricula and a
system of computer-based benchmark assessments for tracking student
achievement. According to the school district, the company has a "more
traditional mathematics program than the district" (District Report, 2007).

The leadership and administration structures were also different at these schools. The schools were broken down into small learning communities (in Bernard's case, two—the 7th grade and the 8th grade), and each team had a lead teacher who worked as "middle management" between the teachers and the administration. In addition, each school had a literacy curriculum coordinator and math curriculum coordinator, who oversaw the implementation and planning of the respective curricula.

The principal kept a tight rein over the school and was concerned with the way that visitors perceived it. This was visually evident in the plethora of school wide concepts and sayings that lined the hall in poster form. A school district evaluation report (2007) also noted that school principals from the company-run schools tended to have strong allegiance and compliance to the company's philosophy, and were outspoken about the positive aspects of the model.

Bernard Middle School has a complex set of structures to facilitate teacher interaction and collaboration. Steven was busy almost every day after school with a meeting or club. He co-taught a class with an inclusion teacher, a class with the math technology teacher, and worked closely with his lead teacher, who coordinated his small learning community, since she shared the same set of students with him. He also met bimonthly with the math curriculum coordinator and attended school professional development trainings at least once a month. Further, post-college volunteers worked at the school as tutors and community program coordinators. In the second half of the year, Steven was assigned a growth teacher, who worked with him as a mentor and advocate.

Though there was a wide variety of supports in place, Steven often felt they were inappropriate for his situation or not available to him. In the beginning of the year, he relied mostly on his lead teacher for support, but found, over the course of the year, that she undermined some of his work with students, and he trusted her less. The math curriculum coordinator would review Steven's progress with the pacing guide and help him keep on track with the curriculum. However, the curriculum coordinator advocated a direct instruction approach, which Steven did not feel was appropriate for his classes. The growth teacher was quite supportive of Steven when she found the time; however, she was very busy. Steven also felt that she approached teaching in a more traditional fashion, what he called "book learning," and he did not. He rarely sought out teaching advice from these formal mentors:

The only thing I really relied on school personnel for was . . .
discipline and how to handle certain situations. Academic? No.
Lesson planning? No. . . . I got really frustrated actually. [In] all our
[Professional Development Workshops]—I just started sitting in the
back of the room, and doing other stuff.

Steven was most engaged in discussions about the curriculum with his co-teachers. He taught one class with a special education teacher and another class with a math and technology teacher (which he initiated). Steven generally took the lead in designing lessons, and his co-teachers shared ideas and input, especially regarding the needs of specific students. The co-teachers were both first-year teachers. Steven appreciated their help, but yearned for advice from an experienced teacher who shared his pedagogical beliefs.

Although the many meetings and emails were sometimes overwhelming to Steven, when the frequency of the communications diminished after statewide testing in the spring, he also noticed how much they had created a buzz of energy in the school; after the tests, teachers met less, talked less, and were less energized to work:

> We haven't had a math department meeting for months now. We meet a little bit in Professional Development, and basically we go over benchmark scores, and [the math coordinator] tells us which section is low, and I'm like, "yeah, that makes sense." [laugh] But . . . we haven't once talked about how to make it through the end of the year. . . . So no real support there. . . .

Although the curriculum was detailed, and there was a complex network of (Traditional) support within the school, Steven still struggled in seeking professional support for his teaching. He felt that his philosophy of teaching did not mesh with most of the people involved in the formal support structure of the school, and he also felt disconnected from the veteran teachers. His most professionally supportive experiences occurred when he co-taught and worked on developing informal relationships.

SOCIAL NETWORKING IN AN
OUTCOMES-ORIENTED SCHOOL CULTURE

Although the approaches to teacher support at Northpoint, Bailey, and Bernard were outwardly different, underneath, the test-oriented school culture provided what the Continuum of New Teacher Support would classify as Traditional support. The strict focus on raising test scores or abiding by specific prescribed practices isolated the new teachers in their attempts to seek out answers to their questions of practice. The schools' stifling of teacher inquiry made it difficult for teachers to actively collaborate and build their social network.

The major lesson to draw from the school descriptions and experiences of teachers in this chapter is in the relationship between the organizational culture of a school, formal structures of support, and support network

NETWORKING TIP

To join an online conversation on schools and teaching led by Teachers College Press authors, visit www.thenetworkedteacher.com/#!community

development. The stories here illustrate what many researchers have noted before—that school culture matters just as much as formal structures and organization (Hargreaves, Earl, Moore, & Manning, 2001; Kardos, Johnson, Peske, Kauffman, & Liu, 2001; Lee, Bryk, & Smith, 1993; Little, 1990). The stories focus on a particular aspect of school culture in relationship to teacher support and networking. This aspect is the locus of support—process (which requires collaboration and teacher inquiry) or product (which situates teachers as the receivers and technicians of work). The locus of support has a direct impact on the networking practices of teachers; it influences their ability to develop support networks, who they see as supportive, their participation in the school community, and their sense of empowerment or professionalism.

However, some teachers succeeded in developing their support networks more than others. Despite the hurdles that some school cultures may place in a teacher's way, all teachers can work to resist or reform the culture and form networks that support their teaching and answer their questions. Schools can also take an active role in fostering teachers' support networks by focusing on teachers' questions and offering support that reflects reform-end characteristics of the continuum. Specific strategies school leaders may take to support network development are described in Chapter 7.

CHAPTER 5

Building Intentional Professional Networks

Over the last 30 years, research on teacher support and induction has developed into a central field of study for education scholars. Much of this research has focused on the efficacy of mentoring and induction programs (Darling-Hammond & McLaughlin, 1995; Feiman-Nemser, Schwille, Carver, & Yusko, 1999; Ingersoll & Smith, 2004). However, the reverse perspective on induction programming has rarely been investigated—that is, who, and what, do new teachers seek for support? Thus far in this book I have begun to answer this question by providing frameworks and examples of new teachers' informal support networks. However, there is an additional question along this line of thought that has yet to be addressed: Of the relationships that teachers develop for support, which ones offer the kind of support that allows the new teacher to be successful, both from a self-efficacy standpoint, and in terms of teacher quality? Here, I begin to answer this question through the stories of two new teachers, Michael and Maria.

As you will see through their narratives, Intentional Professional Networks have a powerful role in providing teachers with a sense of empowerment, emotional support, engagement in teaching, and control over their curricula. Their stories demonstrate findings from previous studies (Anderson, 2010; Baker-Doyle, in press) on the role of Intentional Professional Networks in supporting new teachers. Recall from Chapter 3 that an Intentional Professional Network is:

> A teacher's network of the people they select to collaborate and
> interact with to solve professional problems. Intentional Professional
> Networks are local (most often, in the school), professional
> relationships, formed through active problem solving that result in
> strong ties between the teachers and their Intentional Professional
> Network contacts.

Intentional Professional Networks are the frontline of support for new teachers. They help new teachers to socialize and learn the unwritten rules of the school. They provide Reform-end support to the teachers and value their praxis. Yet, as Chapter 3 revealed, it is common to find a new teacher with an Intentional Professional Network of one or two people.

What happens to teachers with small Intentional Professional Networks? How do new teachers develop robust Intentional Professional Networks? In this chapter we explore these questions and more through the eyes of Michael and Maria, two teachers who taught at the same school, and yet had significantly different experiences in teaching and relating with colleagues. Their stories illustrate the ways in which a teacher's support network and networking behavior can influence their professional identity, commitment, legitimacy, and growth. Michael, who was unsure of who to trust and reach out to, had few individuals in his Intentional Professional Network, and often felt isolated and under attack in school. Maria, on the other hand, was active in collaborating with numerous colleagues at her school, had a large Intentional Professional Network, and gained significant power and professional confidence through her network and activities. This chapter will recount not only the travails and triumphs of their first year, but also of what brought them into teaching, and their beliefs about teaching, which were important factors in shaping their networking characteristics and networks.

MICHAEL CLARK

Michael's first-year story illustrates a teacher's struggles with isolation and development of trust, and how these struggles can impact professional identity and practices. Michael's case is perhaps the most detailed of the four teachers described in this book, because his story illustrates the institutional and personal challenges that can affect network development.

Michael Clark taught 8th-grade general science and 10th-grade biology at Northpoint High School, located in a low-income area of Park City. Urban schools and teaching were quite foreign to Michael, and he approached his practice and interactions from a distance initially; his philosophy was that he was a "performer," on stage for his students. Further, he was wary of building relationships in his school, and he took time to build trusting relationships. He did not have a very high status in the eyes of his school administrators, and was a frequent target of the leadership. Thus, a cycle of isolationism began. It was not until late in the year when he worked collaboratively with a teacher and reached out to students and their parents that he began to feel a stronger sense of teacher identity and professional self-worth.

Background and Teaching Philosophy

Michael, a Caucasian in his early 20s, grew up in a suburban neighborhood on the east coast. He was hired to teach in Park City through the Urban Teacher Program (UTP), an alternative certification teacher program. Teaching at Northpoint was his first full-time career-oriented job since graduating from college the year before. Michael described his first few months in the school as a period of "forced change," in which he was exposed to cultures and experiences that were of "a different world" to him. Michael often fondly recalled his days at college and high school and his strong relationships with teachers. As the year progressed, he struggled to connect these past experiences with his present teaching experiences.

One personal characteristic that Michael discussed frequently in interviews and while he taught was his self-described tendency toward "perfectionism." Michael was unsure if this trait would be a benefit or a disadvantage to his teaching experience. "Impeccability" and "perfection" became driving themes in his practice and inquiry throughout the year.

Michael's perfectionism shaped his teaching philosophy. Early in the year, Michael explained that he believed that the act of teaching was similar to putting on a performance, with the teacher as the actor/director, and the students as actors/audience:

> I see teaching as performance. I am performing every day to an audience. And I have to figure out how best to engage that audience, but also to enable them to become actors in our little play. . . .

As the year progressed, Michael adapted his philosophy to some degree; he felt that there was a greater degree of interaction between the teacher and the students in his teacher-actor theory than he initially believed. In addition, he questioned whether a teacher could maintain a certain performance identity separate from his own.

Goals, Needs, and Challenges

Michael's first year was marked by conflicts with his school administration and shifts in his approach to teaching. When he began the year, Michael was simply overwhelmed by the enormity of the job of a teacher and had difficulty prioritizing where to give his attention. Before he began teaching, he thought of teacher's work as "getting up in front of a group of students and conveying some knowledge or helping them develop a skill." In the classroom, he identified additional roles that he needed to play: "a counselor, and a security guard, a referee, a publisher, a secretary." He felt so overwhelmed by the "volume" of his job that at times he refused support from others because he was "not ready" for it—or felt it did not address his immediate needs. For example, a mentor from his Urban Teaching Program came to help him shape his practice in response to test data from students, yet Michael had placed a low priority on this data entry work, and therefore did not feel this focus was helpful to him.

Beyond managing the many roles of teacher, Michael's two biggest challenges in the beginning of the year were in translating the science curriculum into a format that he and his students could understand and navigating the school social environment. In terms of the curriculum, he was frustrated with the unrealistic objectives of the curriculum text and the complexity of the lesson formats and called the curriculum "flawed." When he sought help from instructors at the university where he took his teacher preparation classes, Michael felt that, again, he was not "ready" for the kind of "big picture" lesson planning help that the instructors provided.

When Michael reflected on the shock of his first few months, he wondered if he would have had the same struggles in a suburban school where he believed he would have an "assumed role." At Northpoint, he could assume nothing—instead, he was distraught with the "sensory, emotion[al] and physical overload" of his job, and noted, "I still haven't settled into an identity yet." In addition, he felt ignored and shrugged off by the administration, and reacted by isolating himself as much as he could from the principal and vice principal. Further feelings of isolation were caused by the fact that he was the only Urban Teacher Program teacher at the school.

Becoming grounded . . . and uprooted. Toward the end of November, Michael seemed to be gradually overcoming some of these challenges. He instituted several routines in the classroom and announced to me that the "tide is turning"—noting that he felt more "like a teacher." In January, he and I sat down to develop a curriculum unit—his first attempt at long-range planning. He spoke of creating "grounded" lessons based on his knowledge of the students' needs and interests. He likened "listening to students" for a positive environment to "listening to your body" for good health. This perspective altered his approach to curriculum development; he would consider what he was "capable of doing" and what he felt that the students needed over what the curriculum guide said to do for the day.

However, Michael's teaching experience shifted dramatically when, in early February, his classroom was broken into and his laptop was stolen. This deeply disturbed Michael for several reasons: The protective "bubble" he had created in his classroom had burst—he was forced to rely on the administration for support and help in the matter, he felt that the trust he developed with his students had dissolved, the curriculum planning he had finally found time to do was destroyed—all the files were on the computer, all his Ivy University work was lost, and his space, which he put so much time and care into, was invaded and damaged. The day after the event, the mood was deadening. Michael had removed all the posters and decorations from his room to emphasize his disappointment. The classroom remained this way for more than a month.

The theft incident brought on a period of conflict and despair for Michael. He desperately tried to get support from administrators to locate the thieves and recover the stolen property, but found himself consumed with school politics and red tape. In addition, he felt his authority had been violated by the vice principal, who had changed his student's grades from F's to D's without his permission.

The wake-up call. This period of despair lasted until an enlightening conversation he had with a student a month later. Ivan, the student, told Michael that he missed the way the room had looked and wondered why Michael expected the students to be "impeccable," when he was not putting in the same amount of effort. For Michael, this conversation was a "wake-up call." He responded by radically changing his approach to discipline and student outreach, organization, curriculum planning, and his interactions with the administration. Michael described his conversation with Ivan and his reaction in a written reflection:

> Mid-March, I spoke with a student of mine . . . who had just started to cut class. I asked him why, and he said that he no longer got a good vibe from my classroom, that he did not feel as though I was trying, and that I no longer expected anything from him. This came as quite a shock, even though I knew it all to be true. After the laptop was stolen, I tried to remove myself in some way from the experience of teaching—tried to pull myself, the human element of myself, out. I subsequently realized that doing so and being a good teacher are mutually exclusive, especially in this environment. . . . I had let them down. I needed to reinvest myself. . . . Shortly after Ivan and I spoke, I put all my things back up and added more. I worked harder to plan engaging lessons/activities. I worked harder to keep my enthusiasm up even when I felt tired or sick. I let go of the anger onto which I had been holding.

It was a moment of self-described enlightenment—Michael had found a "self" in teaching through this student, and it helped him to release some of his performance and perfectionism anxiety.

Michael called the parents of every student in his classes (approximately 90), as well as sent out letters to the parents outlining his expectations for the students. He programmed their phone numbers into his cell phone and called them frequently during class. In class, he redecorated the room, and added posters, graphic organizers, and new quotes. He organized every paper he had and created a new filing and grading system. His approach to the curriculum changed as well; he was once again ready to attempt long-range curriculum planning. In March we worked together to develop another curriculum unit, and he later described the sense of "continuity" that had been built through this project and through his renewed relationships with his students.

In the spring, Michael also began to work with a fellow science teacher, Devon, on cleaning out the old science lab space, which was full of materials, but unorganized and unkempt. Together they spent days and nights cleaning out the room and organizing the materials. Michael ordered animal specimens for dissections and led several popular lab classes over the course of the last month of school. This was perhaps the work that he was most proud of; he fondly noted that when he first started teaching, his students could not be trusted to use eye droppers, and by the end of the year, they were using scalpels to dissect frogs.

Unanswered questions. Toward the end of the year, Michael began to wonder what kind of an impact he had and what kind of teacher he was. As questions dogged him, he also developed physical health problems, spending several days in and out of the hospital. He struggled with the varying perspectives of what a "good teacher" was by his own standards, UTP's standards, and the standards of his colleagues. He also described frustration with the sense of teacher identity, which he felt was mottled by the ups and downs of his year:

> Part of the professionalism of being a teacher is keeping that even keel, regardless of what happens in your room . . . you have to pull yourself out of it, when you feel [upset]. . . . Because in the process of expressing my own emotion, when I'm making something really personal like that, I am destroying a relationship, I'm destroying this connection, I'm hurting the potential learning.

With his students, despite some breakthrough moments, Michael still felt that an emotional barrier was necessary for good teaching—and could actually strengthen a connection between teacher and student. Michael's inquiries drove him to become active over the summer months, developing new curriculum units and reaching out to colleagues and old professors.

Networking Beliefs and Behaviors

Michael felt that he didn't "fit in" at his school. He was the only UTP person at his school, and he also found it difficult to connect with other faculty. Instead he reached for support outside of school, from family and friends. He noted that these long-time friends and relations knew him well and could support him emotionally. For Michael, then, the "fit" was very important; he reached out to people whom he knew would understand his situation and see eye-to-eye with him. Further, Michael often wanted to try things independently before collaborating or reaching out, so he could "learn for himself." When we initially met, I asked Michael how I could support him, as an "action researcher." He replied, "for the most part, I really see you sort of sitting in the background, because I feel like I've got to learn to do this, without the support, I mean that sort of support." As time went by, he became interested in working jointly on unit-planning projects and academic papers.

When Michael wasn't warmed up to the ideas or philosophy of a potential collaborator, he tended to avoid working with him or her. Though he sought support from his UTP mentor and several university instructors, he did not feel their advice was attuned to his interests or needs at the time. The volunteer tutor in his classroom, Tim, noted that he felt his role in Michael's classroom was peripheral; they did not discuss class events or lessons nor did they plan any project together. When Maria organized a collaborative unit among the English, history, science, and social studies teachers, Michael resisted involvement and associated it with administrator control over the classroom. Michael did not feel a strong sense of camaraderie among the teachers at the school, and at times, he referred to himself as being in "self-imposed" isolation from the faculty. Michael wanted to make his classroom a solitary "oasis" in the school.

However, when Michael *did* find a specific reason and the right people to collaborate with, he was quick to reach out. When the vice principal changed his grades unbeknownst to him, he sought advice from Northpoint teachers and university instructors, and even developed a letter-writing campaign, in which he convinced many of the school's teachers to sign a letter reprimanding the vice principal. He sought veteran teachers who knew the system well to get their opinions and advice. Unfortunately, Michael found it difficult to amass support in his favor because he had not developed strong connections to these veterans earlier in the year.

In the spring, Michael gradually began collaborating more with Devon, the other science teacher at the school. By the end of the year, he described her as the person who stood up for him and supported him most. With a year of experience under his belt ("now that I know the right questions to ask"), Michael began to feel more confident about asking others for advice. His plans going into the summer at an end-of-year interview included talking with science content teacher colleagues, grant writing, and "bigger things" that he didn't have time to do during the school year. For Michael, developing an understanding of who was best to work with and what his own interests were was important before he developed new relationships and connections with others.

Michael's Intentional Professional Network and Its Effect on His Teaching

Michael's story highlights the ways in which a teacher's initial hesitance to build a support network inside a school can snowball into greater isolation and detachment from teaching; as Michael built his classroom "oasis," he had more difficulty dealing with administrators, working with the curriculum, and perceiving himself as a teacher, which, in effect, pushed him to isolate himself further. Compared to the three other teachers profiled in this book, Michael had the fewest number of close professional contacts in his school or elsewhere. Only one person in his network, Devon (a teacher at his school), provided strong professional support. He received occasional professional support from me, but I could not meet with him as often as he needed.

Others in his network were mainly family and friends who lived in other locations. They provided mostly empathetic support at a distance. Michael avoided reaching out to administrators or formal support people, because he felt they did not understand what his immediate needs were.

An important person in Michael's network was Ivan, the student who challenged him to meet the same "impeccable" standards as he expected of them. Although students are not often viewed as support persons, in this case, one student's challenge sparked a shift that drove Michael significantly to change his approach to teaching (this kind of support is typical of Diverse Professional Allies, which will be discussed in detail in the following chapter). Toward the end of the year, he became more active in talking and meeting with parents and somewhat more upbeat about his teaching experience, especially the work he did with the science lab.

When Michael began teaching, he was in an environment and a job that was quite unfamiliar to him. There were very few people at his school who knew him well or shared similar past experiences with him, the kinds of people he felt could support him most. As a result, he had a small Intentional Professional Network (only one teacher, Devon). Michael isolated himself at school, in response to several negative experiences and also due to these networking tendencies. He had difficulty establishing a sense of teacher identity, until he worked more intensely with Devon at the end of the year. When he planned lessons, he was frustrated with the curriculum pacing and guidelines, yet he had difficulty figuring out how to develop alternatives and locating the kind of curriculum-planning support that met his needs. Michael was scrutinized by the administration more closely than other teachers, and he often felt under attack. He had very little political power (social capital) in the school. The challenges that Michael faced were related in large part to his lack of professional support contacts in school; and yet, the few people in his Intentional Professional Network and Diverse Professional Ally network (teacher Devon and his student) had a profound effect on helping Michael to overcome these challenges.

MARIA DONNELLY

Maria Donnelly taught 8th- and 10th-grade social studies and history at Northpoint High School. Enthusiastic and outgoing, Maria wore her passion about teaching history on her sleeve; her bookcases were full of copies of primary source documents, history books, and various curriculum guides, and newsprint posters with student group work covered every wall of her room; she hopped from one school committee meeting to another, and declared invariably in interviews and discussions, "I was born to teach!" In class, her students coalesced into groups, which she ultimately designed her teaching style around—an initial class lecture, then independent group work, or discussions. Maria was fascinated with American history, and her interest in gaining expert knowledge in this area drove her to research and design lessons for her classes. She yearned to build an intellectual atmosphere in her classroom and between colleagues at the school. Her biggest challenge in teaching through the year was in incorporating her innovative ideas or plans into the reality of the classroom and school environment.

Though she and Michael taught at the same school (in fact, next door to each other) Maria had a vastly different teaching experience; she referred to her school peers as "family," who "watched her back," and felt empowered in her decisions about curriculum planning and her sense of professional identity. Maria's story is an example of how networks and networking behaviors can reinforce each other and the growth of the teacher's professional status, practices, and identity.

Maria already knew several people in the school district from previous experiences and family relationships, and she reached out quickly to collaborate with a diverse group of people. She did not feel isolated; rather, she felt close with many of the faculty. As the year progressed, the faculty and staff provided support that not only helped her overcome some of her professional challenges, but also empowered her and gave her a very high status with the school administration. Toward the year's end she was considered a school leader, which reinforced her already strong professional identity and her networking behaviors.

Background and Teaching Philosophy

Maria, a Caucasian in her mid-20s, grew up in Park City and attended the public schools in the city. She stayed in the city for college, choosing to attend Ivy University because of its special joint Bachelor's-Master's 5-year teaching degree program. Through the Master's program, she student taught in a Park City public high school, which gave her some background experience using the mandated Base Curriculum. Maria had planned to teach in another state, but after initially being hired, her job fell through, and she returned to Park City to teach the following year.

Maria's mentor relationship and experience with her 11th-grade history teacher convinced her that she should be a teacher. She remained close with her teacher, as well as other friends and family who work in the school district, and often sought support and advice from these individuals.

Maria's philosophy of teaching history and social studies stemmed from her beliefs about teaching high school students. She believed it was important for students to learn to be responsible and how to communicate with people outside of their own community. Part of this goal was related to her beliefs about citizenship. She believed that the purpose of social studies education is to create "good, civic people." To this end, she began the year focusing on the development of specific "skills," such as map-reading, note-taking, and text comprehension. However, toward the end of the year, she shifted her focus to fostering analytic conversations and debates.

This shift in focus could also be observed in Maria's beliefs about and use of the Base Curriculum. Early in the year, Maria said of herself, "I'm a user, I'm not a creator" of the Base Curriculum. She worried about pacing and fitting all the topics into a set period of time. For example, in one interview, she spoke of her frustration to teach several important events in American history over the course of only 4 days to keep pace with the Base Curriculum, including: the Articles of Confederation, the Constitutional Convention, the Constitution itself, and the ratification of the Constitution. Over the course of the year, however, she began worrying less about pacing and becoming more of a creator than a user. This change was sparked by conversations she held with administrators at the school district's social studies curriculum office, who informed her that the curriculum should be considered "more like guidelines, they're not really rules," and told her not to worry about pacing.

Goals, Needs, and Challenges

When Maria began her first year of teaching she was cautious and fearful of taking risks in her interactions with the administration as well as designing the curriculum. The year before, she had been mysteriously laid off from a teaching position, after only 3 weeks on the job. The school informed her that it was due to underfunding, but she suspected it was because she had spoken out too quickly as a new teacher in the school. She explained that she became distinctly aware of a "tenure mentality" in schools from that experience, and compared a first-year experience to "hazing in a college fraternity." Yet, just a few months into the year, Maria became a major risk-taker. She became involved in school leadership projects, experimented significantly with the curriculum, and at times held more power and say about the management of the school than the vice principal or principal. Though she became empowered in many ways through this process, her greatest struggle was in bridging her notions about proper cultural communication and behavior with the beliefs and practices of the students in her classroom.

Initial curriculum fears. In the first 2 months of the school year, Maria's fear of being out of step with the pacing guide in the Base Curriculum caused her to feel as if she didn't have a sense of the bigger goals and questions in the lessons. She planned day-to-day, usually the night before, using the curriculum as her model. In addition to her difficulties interpreting the curriculum, Maria felt that she could not expand upon some of the ideas because of the students' behavior in the class. She did not consider her job to be disciplinarian and was extremely frustrated with the lack of support or programs for students with discipline problems in the school.

Together, these challenges forced Maria to teach in a way that she did not enjoy, nor did she believe wholly benefited her students; Maria often used worksheets as the focal point in these early lessons. Although these practices conflicted with her beliefs about good teaching, she felt limited by the need to adhere to the curriculum pacing guide and to control the students' behavior. Maria began to reach out to colleagues in the school to brainstorm ways to manage student behavior. By the beginning of her second month, she made a friend and ally with a fellow new teacher, Emily Lauer, who taught math at the school. She and Emily met frequently throughout the year to discuss classroom management strategies to address some of the issues that were important to them at the time.

Building bridges and legitimacy. In November of her first year, Maria volunteered to be a department head for social studies, and therefore participated in monthly leadership team meetings with other department heads across the city. She developed a support network of experienced teachers and high-level administrators, who assured her that she did not have to strictly follow the Base Curriculum. When Maria felt she had been given "permission" to "pick and choose" topics to teach out of the Base Curriculum, major changes began to take place in her classroom. This realization sparked a sense of "freedom" for Maria, and she began thinking more about what kind of goals *she* wanted for her students, in addition to the goals of the curriculum. Her continued confidence and development of ideas were sustained by her work with other teachers in the school, particularly Emily Lauer and Matthew Scott. Emily helped Maria to design structures in her classroom that would allow for discussion-based lessons.

Further, Emily helped her to make decisions about what was appropriate material for her class. For example, when Maria was unsure whether she was allowed to show a video in her class, Emily encouraged her to show it, and have confidence in her decision. Matthew introduced new ideas and materials to Maria by bringing in newspaper articles, and encouraging her interests in class conversations. She described her new approach to teaching as "concept based," in comparison to the Base Curriculum's "detail-based" approach (an emphasis on units of information). She quickly discovered that her new approach made her and her students feel more capable and creative, noting:

> When you talk about something like that [issue], and the kids go, "whoa, really?" It just makes me feel like I'm getting more out of the teaching when I do that. And I feel like when I am forced to cover X, Y, and Z in the Base Curriculum, I just get so scared about covering X, Y, and Z, that I don't go above and beyond. I just do what they tell me.

Maria began thinking more about having what she called "open-ended" conversations with her students—intellectual discussions, debates, and group reflections on academic topics. She worked on developing a classroom structure that would allow students to discuss topics openly, yet focus their attention on the topic, and have them behave according to her expectations. She reached out for help from her two classroom volunteer tutors, Tim and Amy, who developed a grading system for pre-class assignments that helped to encourage students to participate, and also assisted during small group work and discussions. As she saw more of what was possible, she also became aware of her intellectual needs as a teacher and began to develop inquiry questions around how to avoid "dumbing down" her lessons. Maria began to reach out even more to colleagues in her school simply to engage in intellectual conversation: to Matthew for international affairs news, and to me to discuss questions about her teaching.

School leadership and power. Parallel to her "liberating" experience with the curriculum, Maria also became highly involved in school leadership and management, which empowered her as a professional and leader. When she realized that the majority of teachers at the school were new (10 out of 16), she felt more comfortable speaking up, because there were few people at the school who had enough tenure to hold a "tenure mentality." Beyond volunteering as a department head, Maria helped to design class schedules, developed a student review and counseling process for failing students, organized an interdisciplinary project among several teachers in the school, and initiated the planning of a graduation ceremony for the last graduates of the school. Her involvement in the leadership team meetings gave her confidence and, in some cases, more authority than her principal and vice principal. If she made a school policy suggestion she was heard and often unchallenged. In June, she conceded, "I have a lot of higher-ups backing me up . . . nobody fights with me."

Networking Beliefs and Behaviors

Maria saw many networking opportunities in the transitional, sometimes chaotic, situation at Northpoint. She described the school's faculty as a "dysfunctional family," which was bonded together in its defiance toward, and struggles with, the administration. She enjoyed being a member of the school's professional community and was proud of what she saw as a collegial atmosphere:

> I feel like I've had, colleague-wise, very positive experiences with everybody I've worked with. I feel like the collegiality, for me, personally, at the school is so open that I can walk down the hallway and I can just have a sparked conversation about, whether it's curriculum, whether it's personal life, whether it's student relations, whether it's teacher relations, and the conversation will just grow, and then you know, we can leave it or we can pick it up later, and everything is very open. And I don't think there's a lot of—well, I think with some people there's a little bit of backbiting, but there's not. I feel comfortable—in my place I'm comfortable with my colleagues.

She was also confident of the support she received from her family and friend networks. She described how family members and friends would call district officials for her to try to locate a teacher coach for the school, and how they gave her early notice of position openings in other schools.

Maria actively searched for people to network with and to support her, often reaching out to particular people for particular types of support. She hung out in the teacher's lounge to meet and talk with teachers, sought out teachers to work on certain projects with her, and strategized with other faculty members as to how to navigate school politics. Below she describes her budding relationship with Emily Lauer, who became a close colleague over the year:

> We sit down and we talk a lot about classroom management stuff because our styles—our styles are different and yet we want the same goal and you know it's just plugging away. I've never called parents before and this is the first year that I've called parents and you know she's used to [it]; when she was doing her student teaching that was like all she did. . . .

Though Emily taught a different subject and had some differences in management style, Maria saw that Emily had several strengths, particularly in working with parents, a practice that Maria knew she needed to learn more about.

Maria would often work with people on targeted questions or specific projects; she had a clear sense of the questions she wanted to ask or the problems she wanted to solve. She partnered with the library teacher on a project that involved technology by showing the teacher her plans and asking whether or not there were any possibilities to collaborate. She called on another math teacher, Mr. Scott, when she wanted to find someone to discuss current events with her. With Emily, she often discussed strategies to cover herself to avoid confrontation with the school administrators.

Another way that Maria built her network was through taking on leadership opportunities in the school. These actions helped Maria to develop strong alliances within the school, a sense of authority, and positive recognition and support from faculty and staff. Maria voluntarily led the development of the individualized instruction plan process along with several other teachers. In doing so, she received praise and support from faculty to surmount numerous bureaucratic difficulties. She reported even more positive feedback after she helped to organize the graduation ceremony for the 8th-grade students, noting that teachers would come to her door, saying, "What can we do to help you?"

This high level of involvement also took a toll on Maria. When she reflected on her first year, she noted that it felt as if it had been a "bogus first year" because of all the work she had to take on to support the school, which took away from the time she could have spent working on lesson planning and designing her classroom. She also felt that the principal considered her an "old hand," and had very high expectations of her. She felt pressure to not make "first-year teacher" mistakes, even though she had no prior teaching experience other than student teaching, and she longed for an experienced teacher to share feedback on her teaching.

There were certain people and groups that Maria tended to avoid or shut out. She did not enjoy visitors to her classroom that could not contribute or support what was happening in the class. When a City Year volunteer was not active enough in her classroom she convinced him to leave, because she felt he was not being useful. She expressed anger when a special education teacher sat in her classroom without supporting or interacting with any students. Maria was also frustrated when the principal brought observers into her classroom who did not offer helpful feedback. In addition, she did not spend a lot of time with students or their parents, in part because of her efforts to maintain discipline. Similar to Michael, she believed that getting on a personal level with students was out of place for school. Yet, contrary to Michael, she felt that the students and faculty behaved "communally" and were supportive. In general, Maria tended to work with a diverse range of people who she sensed would specifically support her, help answer her questions, or lend legitimacy to her leadership.

Maria's Intentional Professional Network and Its Effect on Her Teaching

Maria's story demonstrates the power of an Intentional Professional Network in supporting and sustaining a first-year teacher. Maria had six colleagues in her Intentional Professional Network, the highest number of individuals in the four cases. She also worked closely with two classroom volunteers, Tim and Amy, who became important Diverse Professional Allies. Although Maria was faced with strained relationships with administrators and formal mentors, a curriculum that was difficult to interpret and implement, and a school on the brink of being shut down, she overcame many of those challenges and even felt professionally empowered with the support of people in her networks.

Maria tended to work with diverse groups of people to meet her various needs and often developed close relationships with them. She felt that she was born to teach and networked with others who could help her career at the moment and for the long term. In this way, she reinforced her identity as a teacher by working with people who viewed her in this way and supported her work. When she worked with people in her networks, she often did so through projects and collaborative ventures. These efforts helped her build and nurture her Intentional Professional Network.

Maria started her year fearful of being off-pace with the mandated curriculum, but as she met and worked with others, she quickly realized the degree of control she could have over her classroom and curriculum. She collaborated with many colleagues in the school on classroom projects and also volunteered for several leadership roles. The school administration relied on Maria for her close contacts with the school district, as well as for her work managing the school. Maria acquired a great deal of power and social capital in the school. Maria's intense outreach efforts and cultivation of her Intentional Professional Network and Diverse Professional Ally networks helped to build a strong safety net that aided her through many challenges, and allowed her to pursue her professional goals and interests.

NETWORKING TIP

Who's in your Intentional Professional Network? Use our mapping tools in the appendixes or online at www.thenetworkedteacher.com/#!resources

MICHAEL AND MARIA:
TWO ENDS OF THE SOCIAL NETWORKING SPECTRUM

Maria and Michael's stories represent two very different networks, each on opposite ends of the spectrum. Maria had a large Intentional Professional Network, developed through collaborative projects and active problem solving with others in her school. She worked closely with her classroom volunteers as well. She felt empowered and confident as a result of many of the relationships she developed throughout the year. Michael relied mainly on his friends or parents and out-of-school contacts, who offered distant, often empathetic support rather than professional support. Thus, his Intentional Professional Network was small. In turn, he often felt under attack and was less confident about his teaching and relationships with others.

Michael and Maria's stories are important because they highlight that it is not only important to simply have a support network; it is important to build networks that provide professional support. This requires teachers to *actively* reach out, and *collaborate* with others through multiple venues and approaches, especially *in their schools*. This work is the foundation of building Intentional Professional Networks.

CHAPTER 6

Seeking Diverse Professional Allies

I think initially I went in being afraid of the parents, and then I developed relationships with half of them. And my goal is to develop relationships with 99% of them next year.... I need to continue to work harder towards that value in that classroom.

(Susan Johnson, first-year teacher)

If you were to ask a new teacher about who supports his or her work, rarely would you hear the words "parent" or "community member." Often, for anything beyond disciplinary measures, new teachers pay little attention to these individuals for most of their first year, before they learn to make connections with the nonteaching members of their school communities. Yet, there is great value in these relationships—value that cannot be found through professional development or collaboration with other teachers. What these school community members can offer that other teachers cannot is insight into the students' lives and fundamentally different perspectives on teaching and curriculum. These individuals are what I term "Diverse Professional Allies." They provide new ideas, foster innovation, and, for the teachers, a deeper sense of engagement with students and their curriculum, and they represent the open networks (Cross, Parker, Prusak, & Borgatti, 2003; Gallucci, 2003; Hakkarainen, Palonen, Paavola, & Lehtinen, 2004) discussed in Chapter 3.

Diverse Professional Allies are the most challenging type of network to develop, yet vital to teachers if they want to feel engaged and purposeful in their work. They are challenging because of historical, psychological, cultural, and organizational barriers that prevent new teachers from considering Diverse Professional Allies as sources of support for their teaching. Historically, parents and teachers have been perceived as "enemies" (Lawrence-Lightfoot, 2003), mainly because of a conflict between the parent's interests in his or her individual child, and the teacher's need to value all students equally (which can subjugate the parents' view of their child as unique). However, parents' interests in the outcomes of their child are also a central reason that Diverse Professional Allies are such valuable support people (Strieb, 2010); they are invested in the outcomes of the class, yet they do not mandate particular approaches (as many formal support persons do). Diverse Professional Allies are not just concerned with raising test scores or whether a teacher is strictly following a scripted curriculum; rather, they want the children to be happy and be successful academically. Thus, teachers can seek answers to their questions about their practice in a nonrestrictive way with Diverse Professional Allies, particularly questions about their relationships with the children.

In addition to historical factors, there are also major psychological barriers preventing teachers from perceiving Diverse Professional Allies as support persons. Network researchers have found that individuals are less likely to name people as part of their support network that they perceive to be of lower status (Borgatti & Foster, 2003; Webster, 1995). Further, people tend to gravitate toward others with similar professional backgrounds, status, and race (Hinds, Carley, Krackhardt, & Wholey, 2000). Teachers tend to choose locations to work that reflect the same type of demographic or structural network patterns that they experienced growing up (Boyd, Lankford, Loeb, & Wycoff, 2003). Many of these tendencies can be countered by a more conscious and deliberate approach to developing social support networks. New teachers who are aware of these psychological barriers can participate in teacher research on their own support networks. If a teacher finds that their network seems skewed to their demographic or socioeconomic status, they can take a more active role in developing partnerships or participating in community events to build Diverse Professional Allies.

White teachers need to not only overcome the historical and psychological barriers impeding partnership with Diverse Professional Allies, they also need to work effectively with African-American families and other minorities, which has been documented as a challenge to many White teachers (Howard, 1999). Alternatively, African American and Latino teachers might find themselves working in a school where the majority of students are South Asian; they, too, would need to learn about and work with people with different cultural backgrounds and perspectives than their own. Sometimes a teacher's reluctance to work with Diverse Professional Allies is an obvious discomfort with or ignorance of others' cultures. Most times, this disinclination is subtler, represented as a worry that a parent "wouldn't understand" or that a community member "isn't interested." This factor is also one that must be uncovered through teacher research and close attention to behaviors and interactions with school community members.

Finally, a combination of the latter factors affects the social and organizational structures of urban schools today. Parents and community members are typically thought of as separate or secondary; the school community seed as the teachers, students, and administrators. Organizationally, there are often only token gestures of parent or community participation in the school, such as an open house night or a winter performance. More subtly, school leaders tend to emphasize a focus on the curriculum and test preparation rather than building relationships with the broader community. These are school socialization and organizational factors that can train a new teacher to ignore the prospects of Diverse Professional Allies as support persons.

In this chapter you will read the stories of two teachers, Susan and Steven, who faced many of these obstacles but found ways to overcome them. Their stories demonstrate the effect of Diverse Professional Allies on their teaching and classrooms. Susan's story of radical transformation from struggling day-to-day teaching a scripted curriculum to creating her own peace-themed curriculum, and collaborating with parents and community organizations, shows the ways in which Diverse Professional Allies can shift negative thinking and empower a teacher. Steven's story is also a tale of transformation and engagement, as well as a journey of discovery of self and social justice.

SUSAN JOHNSON

Susan Johnson was a teacher torn between following the status quo to be accepted by the teacher community at her school and get their support, and following her own professional instincts about her students' needs and what good teaching practices were. This conflict impacted her networking behavior; though she wanted to work with many people at the school, she had difficulty in acculturating herself to the school norms because she did not share the philosophies of many of the teachers. As a result, she worked closely with only a few teachers at her school. Yet these teachers were engaged with the parent community in the school, and their efforts to help Susan connect with the parents and her students (her Diverse Professional Allies) acted as a catalyst for her personalization of the mandated curriculum and changes in professional identity.

Background and Teaching Philosophy

Susan, a tall Latina first-year teacher, taught 4th grade at Bailey Elementary school. Though she towered over her students, she had a youthful appearance and dressed stylishly, with an urban professional wardrobe. To Susan's students, she presented herself as calm, somewhat stern, and serious about learning; she followed the mantra "don't smile until Christmas." To colleagues in the school, she let down her guard a bit and tried to be more outgoing, even when she didn't feel comfortable. Early in the year, Susan was not sure how to develop relationships with other faculty, but she grew confident and secure by June after developing strong friendships with a few teachers at the school. Susan wanted desperately to be disciplined in her approach to teaching and managing the students; she dissected the scripted curriculum and asked always, "What is the *right way* to do it?" Susan worried that she would be reprimanded for not following certain grading processes or curriculum policies in the school. Her room was decorated by many colorful, hand-drawn posters that indicated the rules for reading and writing, test-taking tips, mathematical equations, and schedules for the day. For most of the year, student work was rarely posted; this was a stressful project for Susan, because it required her to step outside of the boundaries of what she *knew* was "acceptable" within the school.

Susan began her year feeling somewhat bewildered about what was not only acceptable to the school, but what she really thought about teaching. When asked about her philosophy of teaching in the beginning of the year, she said simply, "all students can learn." Yet by the end of her first year, she developed a far more complex pedagogy and praxis—surprising herself and others with the passion she had about her beliefs, which were rooted in social justice and inquiry. In some ways, Susan's evolution and change of praxis was more intense than the three other teachers described in this book. Many of these changes were tied to her work outside of school—with parents, students, and community members.

Goals, Needs, and Challenges

Susan disliked teaching for the first few months of her job. She wanted to follow the rules of the school: teach the mandated curriculum, socialize in the correct way, understand and speak in the discourse of the professional culture at the school. However, she just did not feel like she fit in. Her ideas did not sync with the curriculum, and she never had time to learn about the students. Susan did not like the way most of the teachers talked about the students, and she wanted to find people who could talk with her about professional matters, not personal issues. She began to question if this was the right job for her.

When Susan became more involved with fellow teacher Sharon Korman and the community-based City Singers choir program, she saw an alternative conception to teaching—and she liked it. The program valued students for more than their academic ability. She got to know students whom she had considered "lost causes" on a level that was deeply emotional and endearing. Susan talked with Sharon about the students and her work in respectful, professional ways. She spent a lot of time with students and their families outside of school. Susan discovered that when she viewed herself as a caregiver, rather than a stern evaluator, she liked what she saw:

> I hated teaching—the first four months of teaching. . . . And now . . .
> I've really enjoyed teaching; I've remembered why it was that I wanted
> to do this for a while in my life. . . . The kids that hated me, in the
> very beginning, [now] I'm like their mom. It's incredible, like how they

respect me, the way that—I must have had 20 people in the
last month come up and tell me, "your class has changed so
much, the way that they act, the peace that they have, the ways they
behave,". . . and the children that people advised me to ignore,
are now actually progressing academically and socially . . . they're just
wonderful. (Susan, Interview, 2007)

Although the school culture and organization acted as a barrier for Susan
in the beginning of her year, her involvement with the community through
an established program helped her to develop a strong network of Diverse
Professional Allies.

Changes in curriculum. Susan had difficulty incorporating her own
ideas and plans into the mandated curriculum. She felt there was not enough
time to do the extra activities she was interested in because of the tight
schedule enforced by the curriculum. She was also challenged in helping
to build a sense of community in her classroom. Throughout the year, an
underlying theme in all of her own lessons and activities was about peace:
"I want to have like a culture of peace within my classroom" (Susan, Interview, 2007), she noted. She had the students make peace poems, and discussed peace frequently with them.

In the first half of the year, her attempts brought about a great deal of
frustration. She felt that they talked about peace often, but the students still
fought frequently and didn't understand the true meaning of the word. A
critical moment in Susan's teaching experience occurred when she introduced the Peace Wall to her classroom, and her students began to understand and reflect the "peaceful" talk she had encouraged all year.

The Peace Wall was a public acknowledgment of peaceful acts made
by the students. The students met together at the end of the school day and
reported on each other's (*not* their own) peaceful acts. This provided a space
for the students to critically examine their ideas about what peace was,
rather than receive a lecture from Susan, and share more about their lives
than they had been able to before:

Sometimes when we're making comments, . . . I'm just like, "okay, well
how is that showing peace?" or if a lot of them say, "somebody says
thank you, somebody said thank you," and somebody was grateful or
something like that then I challenge them to think deeper about some
other things that we do that show peace. There are a billion different
ways to be peaceful. Let's think of more . . . than their examples.

After the creation of the Peace Wall, Susan began to see real changes in
the students' conceptualization of peace and felt empowered by the shift:

"I'm actually doing something that is worthwhile, and it is rubbing off on them, because we talk about peace and gratitude like every single day."

Susan learned about the idea of a Peace Wall from Sharon Korman, who had visited another school that had one as a school-wide project. Sharon, a provider of Reform support, supported Susan in her promotion of peace, and helped to extend Susan's peace projects through incorporating the ideas into her music class. When Susan's class made peace poems, Sharon had one of her music volunteers help transform them into songs. The children sang their songs at a community event, which most parents attended. This event provided a chance for parents to discuss and hear the work the children had been doing in class. It established an ongoing dialog between Susan and the parents about her work on the peace theme, and she developed a discourse with them through the project that aided in classroom management, student engagement, and communication.

From lost cause to found cause. The choir program was central to Susan's turnaround in her belief in herself and her ability to relate her work to her students. In fact, similar to Michael's student, one student became a catalyst for Susan to rethink her assumptions about teaching. For the first several months of teaching, Susan struggled with one of her students, to the point of giving up. In fact, she mentioned several times that other teachers in her school called him a "lost cause," or said that he was "long gone." Although something didn't sound right about these assessments, Susan started to believe it herself after many months of trying to have him stay on task and behave according to school expectations.

In February, the choir had its first community concert after school. Susan assumed her "lost cause" would not show up, because he was usually unreliable with his homework and late to school. One minute before the bus started to depart for the concert hall, he appeared, alone, without a chaperone (all students were supposed to bring an adult chaperone). Susan was worried about this, so she told him that she would have to be his "pretend mom" for the night. At that moment, something changed for him and Susan. He sat close to Susan the whole night, saved her seat, picked up a snack for her, helped her distribute papers, and enamored his teacher with his care and concern for her that night.

The mutual trust and caring did not end on that night. Susan felt enormously guilty for listening to teachers who wrote him off as a failure, and she used this lesson to develop a stronger relationship with him (and others) the rest of the school year. She spent time with him after school, some on his schoolwork, and sometimes just reading to him or talking. He, in turn, became an ally in the classroom, looking and listening and learning. In June, Susan reflected that the student would always have a "special place in [her] heart." Indeed, he would also have a special place in her praxis.

Networking Beliefs and Behaviors

When Susan began teaching at Bailey, she was eager to reach out to teachers to learn from them and collaborate with them. She quickly learned that, within the Bailey school culture, if she wanted connections with teachers she would have to prove herself as a teacher before gaining legitimacy with the faculty and gaining their trust. So, Susan changed her strategy. Instead of asking others for help, she learned what they wanted from her and preformed the tasks and work necessary to gain approval in their eyes. This was a survival strategy for Susan—in her small school, she absolutely needed the community to accept her. However, it was not her support-seeking strategy. These teachers did not offer the professional support that Susan needed— their support was Traditional in nature. To locate support, Susan began looking for the few teachers who shared her pedagogical beliefs, and eventually also sought out parents and students for support and inspiration.

It was one incident in the beginning of the year that taught Susan the Bailey ways. She needed help trying to figure out how to do the writing assessment. No one that she asked had time to help her, so she went to the principal instead. This broke a major social more at the school—going above a senior teacher's head. Susan was exiled from the community until she started to "play politics," which included giving compliments, attending social lunches, and conforming to school mores. Soon, she began to "earn points" in her favor and, as she developed her personal craft of teaching, was more accepted into the community.

Although midway through the year the community accepted Susan more, Susan did not feel it offered valuable support. Sharon Korman and one or two other teachers in the school made up her Intentional Professional Network. Yet, what she lacked in an Intentional Professional Network, she made up for in her Diverse Professional Allies. She regularly talked on the phone with "about half" of the parents of students in her class, attended students' sports games after school, and spent time one-on-one with students during her time off. In addition, she sought support from colleagues outside of school as well as past professors and relatives.

Susan's Diverse Professional Ally Network and Its Effect on Her Teaching

Susan's Diverse Professional Ally Network was the most robust of all the teachers described here. Similarly, her radical change in approach to teaching and beliefs about students surpassed the others. There is a relationship between these two factors. Diverse Professional Allies—parents, students, and community members—help teachers to think innovatively and keep the child in mind. Susan's curricular innovations, understandings of the students' needs, and her feelings of efficacy in teaching all stemmed from these relationships. She did not initially realize or appreciate the value of DPAs, and it took a teacher from her Intentional Professional Network and participation in community programs to develop these connections. With DPAs, new teachers may need help to establish these connections initially—it can be confusing and, to some, bewildering. At the end of her year, when Susan was asked about her philosophy, it was not a thought, but an action—to develop relationships with more parents in her classroom the next year.

STEVEN CARLSON

Steven's story is similar to Susan's because he was often torn between what he was told was right, and what he believed was right. In Steven's case, he was torn three ways—between the school, his beliefs, and the guidance he received from his Urban Teaching Program (UTP—the same alternative teaching program in which Michael participated). Also, like Susan, Steven tried to take advantage of every opportunity to network, yet was stymied in doing so. Steven's networking was affected, however, by somewhat different factors. Instead of the inherent Traditionalist school culture that drove Susan to limit her Intentional Professional Network, it was the standardized data-driven orientations of Steven's school and the UTP that made networking difficult for Steven. By thinking outside of the box he began connecting with students and teaching in a way he felt was meaningful and just.

Background and Teaching Philosophy

Steven, a Caucasian man in his late 20s, taught 7th-grade math at Bernard Middle. He had a busy, gregarious manner. A few years older than most UTP teachers, Steven entered UTP after a short career in the television film industry. Though he rarely incorporated his knowledge of film and video into the classroom, his previous work experience shaped his work ethic and perspectives. He was used to long nights in the editing room so he was not alarmed at the notion of staying past six o'clock at night to work at school. He was, however, challenged by the "teacher personality" that was expected of him by the school and UTP; he felt they encouraged authoritarianism and strict discipline, whereas he wanted to learn how to have more sociable relationships and atmosphere in his classroom. In addition, he became confused and conflicted when the expectations he initially had about learning and curriculum development did not emerge as realistic or reflect his goals for the students.

At Bernard School Steven was surrounded by academic messages and mantras (for example, "Work Hard. Be Nice. No Excuses," "Did I Do Everything to Receive a 4?" and "Every Action Has a Consequence"), which he incorporated both physically around the room (in posters and pictures), as well as in his language and teaching. Through the year, Steven became more selective about what messages and mantras he believed in, and which ones he wanted to share with his students. Like Susan, Steven became conflicted with much of the philosophy and pedagogical practices at his school; yet perhaps because the school mantras were top down rather than socially engrained, he had a broader network of less formal professional support contacts in his school. During his first year, Steven changed his use of the curriculum and his conceptualizations about working with students as he learned more about students' lives outside of school.

Goals, Needs, and Challenges

Steven did not have a lot of prior training or experience with curriculum development and lesson planning, nor did he feel he had access to adequate support for this matter in his school. He felt challenged by lesson planning and delivery; he knew there was something not working but he wasn't sure how to fix it, noting, "I know there are certain things I'm not doing, like, I'm not connecting it to what they know or their actual lives enough, and that's a problem. I'm doing too much talking." His challenges with curriculum development also contributed to problems with classroom management. He described the curriculum he was assigned to use by his school as, "dry . . . it never relates to like students lives, barely. Or ever. . . . [And] it assumes students know everything at all on grade level."

Within the school, Steven found that his formal support contacts were often too busy to help him with planning, or didn't share his views on teaching. Steven also had access to support from UTP and his City University courses, but, as he noted, they rarely focused on curriculum design; rather, the focus was more on raising test scores:

> We talked about trying to stay on pace: . . . you pre-test your students
> and you look at objectives they're at, between like 40% and 60%, and
> you say, okay, I'm going get all my students above 80% so . . . that's all
> UTP gave me.

Steven's most significant source of curriculum support came from his co-teachers. They helped him plan and think about how to relate the content to the students. However, both of his co-teachers were first-year UTP teachers and struggled with similar issues and questions as Steven. On reflection at the end of the year, Steven realized that he needed support from someone at the beginning of the year to tell him it was okay to be off pace and work from where his students were, instead of just saying, "No! 7th-grade math starts now!"

Steven's self-identified "big challenge" was discipline. As he realized that this issue was connected to his development of lessons and curriculum, he began to reject much of the prescribed pacing system and assignments.

He began to look online for math problems and activities that he could assign to his students and worked with UTP colleagues for math instruction support. Although he was still focused on test scores, he decided that his ideas and methods, based on his knowledge of the students, were more effective than the curriculum guides.

Teamwork. Steven's struggles with discipline were his main concern for the first 6 months of the year, with little change and intermittent support from his growth teacher and lead teacher. When Steven decided to team up with Daphne, the science teacher who taught the same group of students, they developed an ambitious, last-ditch plan to call all of the parents of the students in their classrooms. Through this activity, he learned about the lives of the students and was able to disconnect a bit from the school mantras and structures to think about their lives in the world outside of school. Steven noted,

> Next year I plan on doing my home visits before school starts. . . .
> I need to have that positive and that relationship built up way before school even starts because I think it's easy for me to blame them, "oh these kids you know at home haven't been trained to sit down." That's not it. . . .

In talking with the parents, Steven learned how invested they were in their children, and he began to realize how important they were as allies and information providers. His barriers to making these connections went beyond the social structures; there were underlying cultural barriers that made it difficult for him to understand students' and parents' behaviors. In reflecting on the changes he had undergone through the year as a teacher, Steven noted that this conceptualization of the importance of parents was the major shift in his philosophy of teaching, and he felt it strengthened him as a professional.

Surprising defiance. The conceptual connections that Steven made between student behaviors, pacing, curricula, and student needs jolted him to step out of the comfort zone of routine and conformity. In fact, like Maria, he presented a kind of fearlessness of going off pace to meet the students' needs. In his final interview, Steven spoke of being unafraid to tell the principal what he was and wasn't going to teach, depending on what students needed at the time. This realization did not come from a big moment such as Susan's choir encounter with her student. It came in small moments, such as watching students feel successful when they incorporated rap music into learning math equations, learning about the troubled home life of one of his students from a paraprofessional, and thinking about how to connect his prior experiences in television production with the teaching of mathematics.

The result, however, was similar to Susan's change in her praxis—his central philosophy of teaching became wrapped in a strong belief in connecting with parents and students.

Networking Beliefs and Behaviors

Steven did not hesitate to call for help when he had a problem. Perhaps because of his personality, or his prior experience in a fast-paced, people-oriented career, he had no qualms negotiating with the administration to receive more support. Steven's persistence to communicate was not dissuaded by the administration—it was encouraged. When Steven decided to email everyone on the eight-person leadership team each time that a student committed an infraction in his classroom, for documentary purposes, he remarked that his assigned mentor teacher said, "I think it's good you're sending out those emails—it's showing your leadership team that you are trying harder."

Despite Steven's industrial networking style and responsive formal support network, he had difficulty finding many people who he considered suitable to help him with his biggest challenges: classroom management and designing lessons and curricula. When Steven looked to the veteran teachers at his school he found that they did not share his teaching philosophy. Steven attended math department meetings and even led the Math Club, but the department meetings focused more on pacing and test score–raising strategies than content, and the curriculum coordinator was a proponent of "direct instruction," which did not suit Steven's pedagogical beliefs. He observed his lead teacher (a cross between administrator and teacher), who had great classroom management skills and shared his students, but she undermined his authority and lost his trust. Out of ideas, but desperate for support, Steven turned to his UTP colleagues, all first-year teachers who worked in other schools. UTP made space for him to foster peer relationships, and he took advantage of the opportunity, in part because of his networking personality. However, many of these teachers were feeling just as lost as Steven.

Steven's decision to make phone calls with his co-teacher was an important point in his network development. He began to value parents and students as valuable classroom allies. They responded quickly (sometimes too quickly—one father came to the school within 5 minutes of being called). Yet Steven was surprised that neither the school nor UTP offered support or training in developing relationships with parents. He recalled that over the summer he attended a diversity training, which encouraged him to empathize with urban students, but never showed him how to actually develop connections. It was only by the process of observing, working with, and reaching out to students and parents that Steven began to see the central role that Diverse Professional Allies played in his search for support.

NETWORKING TIP

Who are the people in your teaching neighborhood? Map it out or learn more about developing your Diverse Professional Ally network at www .thenetworkedteacher.com/#!resources

Steven's Diverse Professional Ally Network and Its Effect on His Teaching

When Steven began teaching he actively searched for support, but the support he found to teach the prescribed curriculum just did not seem to fit his needs (or his students' needs). The support available to him was primarily Traditional or outside of school. His questions during this time period were, "How can I raise students' test scores?" and "How do I keep on track with the pace of the curriculum?" It was his work with Diverse Professional Allies that pushed him to develop more inquiry-oriented questions, such as "How can I develop this curriculum to meet my students' needs and interests?" and "What engages my students in learning?" In turn, these questions challenged him to re-examine the way he used his curriculum, prompting him to take a stronger decision-making role in its implementation.

COMMUNITY MEMBERS AS CATALYSTS

Susan and Steven's stories are hopeful stories of change. Although initially they did not realize the role that parents and community members could play as catalysts, support people, and innovators, they understood their tremendous value by the end of the year. They overcame many barriers, and they had help—in each case, another teacher introduced them to the idea of working with and listening to the community. The lessons here are not just for new teachers, who now know the challenges and the values of developing Diverse Professional Ally networks, they are also lessons for experienced teachers and mentors, who can help as gatekeepers and boundary-crossers (both network terms for people who help others make connections).

CHAPTER 7

Social Networking for Teachers, Teacher Educators, and School Leaders

In previous chapters, I examined the research and theory behind social networks, discussed the ways schools can impact teachers' networks, and described the stories of four first-year teachers and the social networks that shaped their experiences. These descriptions showed how Intentional Professional Networks and Diverse Professional Ally networks can help new teachers to locate emotional, social, and material resources; develop a social and cultural awareness of the school and its community; and foster innovation and student-centered teaching. Although Maria, Michael, Susan, and Steven's stories told of the development of their social support networks, these first-year teachers did not know the theories of social networks and did not consciously strategize to build their support networks with these notions in mind. In this final chapter, I describe ways that new teachers can take a more active and conscious role in their network development, pushing past the common barriers that beginning teachers face in finding support. Further, I identify actions that teacher educators, formal teacher networks, and school leaders can take to help new teachers develop their networks.

IDENTIFYING NEEDS AND CONTEXT

The first step in consciously developing a support network is for new teachers to reflect on their challenges, needs, and the school environment in which they work. As discussed previously, certain kinds of networks are better for addressing particular needs. For example, a teacher who feels uninspired or disconnected from their curriculum may benefit from developing stronger partnerships with parents and community members (reach out to Diverse Professional Allies). Conversely, a teacher who is having trouble navigating the politics of their school may do well to collaborate with a few teachers at their school to develop their networks (build their Intentional Professional Networks). Thus, before examining new teachers' networks, the teachers must first identify what kinds of support best suit their needs.

Many times teachers note that they have difficulty identifying particular needs; everything seems overwhelming to them. In cases such as these, it may be beneficial for the teacher to identify a specific incident or interaction that was particularly challenging or upsetting, and begin to examine the core issue of the incident to begin with. Michael, for example, could have focused on the stolen laptop issue. Beyond developing a mistrust of his students, he was most upset with the reaction from the administration and faculty (their lack of compassion). Therefore, the core issue for this particular incident was the difficulty of relating to others in the school. Strategically thinking, Michael should then consider developing his Intentional Professional Network.

Another issue to consider before delving into network examination or development is school context. Some school cultures make it difficult for new teachers to seek support due to organization, guiding ideologies, or school culture. As a result, teachers' efforts to develop their networks as they would like them may be stifled. For example, Susan's school culture favored isolation and privatism. However, such barriers can be overcome. Susan had a smaller, more intense Intentional Professional Network in her school and a broader alliance of Diverse Professional Allies outside of school; she worked around the barriers to strengthen her network where she could. Another method is to take a more active role in challenging the school culture or ideology: Offer out-of-school opportunities for colleagues to spend time with you, focusing on your questions of teaching. Many teachers participate in teacher-run support networks outside of school, such as a local chapter of the National Writing Project. These networks can be very helpful to teachers, especially those who have difficulty building Intentional Professional Networks in their own school.

DISCOVERING A SOCIAL SUPPORT NETWORK

Once beginning teachers have reflected on their context and needs, they should then take a close look at their current support network. To map out a network, teachers should first simply list all the people they see as supporting or influencing their teaching. Once this list is developed, each network member should be described in terms of their demographics, their type of relationship to the teacher (friend, colleague, administrator, etc.), their location, the intensity of support they provide, and the type of support they provide (according to the Continuum of New Teacher Support). If it is helpful, the network can be drawn out as the map below (Figure 7.1), so that it is easy to identify the roles and identities of individuals in the support network (Appendix B also includes a template for a network map, or go online at

Figure 7.1. Social Network Sample Diagram

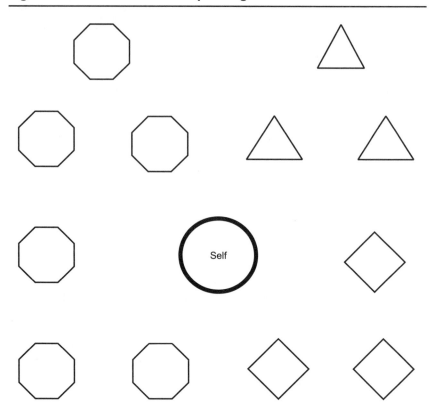

www.thenetworkedteacher.com/#!resources to create an interactive map). Also, the teacher should note any organizations or groups that he or she is involved with that support his or her teaching.

Once the network is identified, it should be examined for network characteristics. Who offers the most intense support? Could it be described as professional support? Are the individuals part of the teachers' Intentional Professional Networks, Diverse Professional Allies, or neither (perhaps friends or family?). Who offers less support? Is there a group not represented in the network (for example, no Diverse Professional Allies)? Is the teacher involved in any support groups? Summarize the trends of the network—compare them to other new teachers. Look closely for connections between the challenges that the teacher faces and the patterns in the network. This process will highlight the strengths and weaknesses of a new teacher's network. Once the weaknesses have been identified, teachers can take steps to strategically developing their networks for greater support.

DEVELOPING INTENTIONAL PROFESSIONAL NETWORKS

There are two essential concepts to understand before developing an Intentional Professional Network. First, an Intentional Professional Network is developed through *action*—teachers who collaborate with each other develop different kinds of relationships than teachers who have lunch together. The most intense professional support comes from people who are equally invested in the outcomes of a project as the new teacher—they work together on a project or inquiry. Susan's story illustrates this principle well. She was "forced" to eat lunch with the other teachers in her school to survive socially; within the school culture, lunchtime chatter was considered positive socialization—yet collaboration was viewed more negatively. However, Susan developed a deep friendship and relationship with the colleague that she collaborated with on the city choir program. She enjoyed spending time with this teacher and perceived her as a major support person.

The second concept that is important to Intentional Professional Network development is that new teachers need to seek support on answers to *their own questions*—not the questions of others. For example, joint lesson planning is not going to be helpful to a new teacher if they are working on a scripted curriculum that does not reflect their students' needs and interests. It may, however, be helpful if the teachers take an inquiry stance with the curriculum, to investigate how to develop the curriculum to meet their students' needs and interests. This contrast is exhibited in Maria and Michael's stories. Michael was frustrated in lesson planning with the other science teacher because they were simply planning from the book, and he gave up quickly. Maria, however, enjoyed working with the math teacher to develop a classroom management system that worked for both of them. They collaborated throughout the year.

Thus, to build an Intentional Professional Network, new teachers need to collaborate with teachers on projects and inquiries that are important to them. However, for many teachers, time is a major issue. New teachers spend much of their time planning, trying to figure out paperwork, and setting up their classroom (as well as often attending induction programs throughout the year). What is a new teacher to do? A beginning teacher needs to be realistic with his or her time. It certainly makes sense to develop individual collaborations with one or two teachers in their school, but they can extend their network through participation in groups of colleagues. Although some might argue that new teachers should steer away from school committees, teacher groups, and leadership roles, I posit that participation in one or two groups allows teachers to develop a wider network than possible with individual relationships. Such groups may meet once or twice a month but can foster relationships that give continued support to a new teacher. Though a first-year teacher, Maria joined the social studies committee for her district and was greatly empowered through the network she developed via this activity.

There are several kinds of groups in schools that a new teacher can participate in to develop their Intentional Professional Network. First, school leadership and committee work is a good way to build relationships with school leaders and administrators and get a sense of the school culture and goals. Second, teacher inquiry groups inside a school can give new teachers the opportunity to discuss their practice and meet other inquiry-minded teachers. Third, nonprofessional groups (for example, book clubs) allow teachers to meet a more diverse range of individuals from their school in a less threatening environment, which may help to shift school culture, if this is a challenge. New teachers can also become involved with professional networks outside of school and try to invite one or two teachers from their school along to have a shared experience. Although these sound like a lot of effort and time, teachers who participate in groups such as these often say that they couldn't do without them; they offer invaluable community and ongoing support.

DEVELOPING DIVERSE PROFESSIONAL ALLY NETWORKS

We know that it is difficult for new teachers to develop Diverse Professional Allies, and that often they are not even acknowledged as a source of support. Thus, I suggest three major methods of developing a Diverse Professional Ally, and teachers can participate in varying levels for each method. The first method I call *Presence*. Teachers, regardless of their experience level, often enter and leave their school building and rarely venture into the neighborhood. Those that do spend time in the community become known as the go-to teachers—the ones who can help, and who should be supported. When new teachers begin their work at a school, one thing that they can do is to learn about the major community and afterschool programs in the area and visit a few. Teachers can ask their students about their activities after school and on weekends to learn of these organizations, or talk with other members of the school community. Spending out-of-school time in the neighborhood shows parents and community members that a teacher is invested in the community. Further, the students do not leave the area in the summer (other than for vacation), and this is a good time for teachers to be engaged in the community without worrying about the time crunch. Teachers can participate in formal community programs if they are interested, but it is not a necessity. What is important is to be a presence in the community.

The second method is *Family-Centered Curriculum*. As the name suggests, this method integrates the stories, experiences, and lives of the students' family members into the curriculum. It is important for new teachers to communicate with parents before the start of the school year, and to ask them to complete an inventory about their child and their family. This inventory can help teachers develop a curriculum that involves family members. For example, if the teacher notices that many parents share a similar type of job, the teacher incorporates it into a unit theme. Also, of course, teachers can invite parents and community members in to share their stories and talents. Further, beginning the year with a unit on family stories or family history (and involving the parents in the telling) can help launch relationships and show the parents they are invited into the class. Parents and community members should be recognized frequently for any participation they have with the class. Teachers may choose to work closely with one parent in organizing an event or demonstration and, of course, welcome parent volunteers into the classroom. This method helps to engage parents and community members in the curriculum, and helps the teacher to learn more about the community.

The third method, *Broadcasting*, relates closely to Family-Centered Curriculum. This method involves sharing news of the class with the community. Technology can be helpful with this method—teachers can develop a blog to share classroom events, which also allows parents to respond and discuss the events. A newsletter is central to this method. Newsletters are not just for announcements. They can share children's work and discussions, describe crafts, recipes, and songs used in class, and let students share their voices. The important idea behind the newsletter is that the teacher finds a way to let the receiver experience a bit of the classroom. One step beyond a newsletter is workshops. A teacher can offer parents workshops on how to help their children with reading or math, or simply to discuss common parenting issues. This gives the teacher a chance to explain some of the work they've done in their class and to listen to parents' questions and concerns.

Presence, Family-Centered Curriculum, and Broadcasting are three general methods for building relationships and support with parents and the broader community. Teachers can get creative with these methods or use what works for them in their situation.

NEW TEACHERS FACING COMMON CHALLENGES

There is a range of challenges that new teachers face in developing support networks for their practice. Some have been mentioned already—school culture and organization, tension with parents, and lack of knowledge of the community or cultural practices. In addition to these issues, the personality of a teacher can affect how he or she interacts with others, and lack of time to collaborate can isolate a teacher. There are a number of strategies new teachers can use to face these challenges. Each strategy represents a concerted effort to push past the obstacles that stand in the way of support network development, which we know is vital to the new teacher.

School culture and organization have been discussed frequently in this book because they have a major impact on support networks, especially Intentional Professional Networks. I have mentioned that teachers may seek to strengthen the aspects of their support network that they can and participate in formal teacher networks as a source of support. In addition, teachers can seek support from professionals in other schools or organizations, as long as they have a thorough understanding of the context in which the teacher works; an understanding of context is key to providing a new teacher with professional support. Some teachers may choose to take a more active role in changing the organization or culture of their school. This can begin with requesting an altered schedule, to allow for more time for collaboration, and continue with organizing inquiry groups and collaboration. This type of activism requires knowledge of the pedagogical interests of faculty in the school, which can be achieved through smaller collaborations, discussions, and observations.

Cultural differences and perceptions of parents can also hinder network development. In addition to practicing the Diverse Professional Ally–building methods, one strategy to help overcome communication barriers is to have the new teacher work with a *boundary crosser*—someone who has a foot in both the school and community, and is willing to help the teacher make connections with parents and community members. Also, new teachers may be unaware of some of the fears or assumptions they have about the community or their students. Engaging in teacher inquiry and reflection can help new teachers realize where their own perceptions may act as stumbling blocks in their network development.

It may not be biased perceptions of others that hinder a new teacher from reaching out to others—it could simply be that they are shy or unaccustomed to collaborating professionally with others. For these teachers, the first strategy might be to find the *connectors* (Gladwell, 2002) at a school—the people who are extremely outgoing and willing to help a new teacher socialize. These individuals may not have the same pedagogical beliefs or offer professional support, but they can act as bridges within the school community for shy teachers to begin building a support network. A second strategy is to participate in formal groups. Often teachers that have difficulty developing relationships can at least get to know others through formal groups such as committees or councils. Third, teachers can use technology to develop deeper relationships and collaborate if face-to-face communication is difficult. If, as the old proverb goes, "the mountain won't come to Mohammed, Mohammed must go to the mountain," teachers that have difficulty reaching out can give others reasons to reach out to them by sharing news of their work and their classroom through newsletters, visual displays, and technological publications. Finally, one strategy that all new teachers can use, whether they are shy or an extrovert, is to tell people when they need help—keeping silent will only exacerbate any struggles; in most cases, people know new teachers need help and are willing to help them if asked.

The last major concern of teachers in developing support networks is time. Time is the most valuable currency in teaching—and teachers are thrifty, in this case. The best way to overcome the challenge of lack of time is for new teachers to integrate collaboration and outreach into their day. Planning becomes planning together (remember, though, only if the teachers' questions and interests are at heart), grading becomes collaborative grading—and perhaps a time for inquiry about one or two students, and dismissal time becomes a time to talk with parents about upcoming activities. However, it can be difficult for a new teacher to manage all this while learning to teach. Additional strategies are to seek support online—particularly with teachers or community members who know your teaching context—and to dedicate a set amount of time per week (1 hour, for example) toward collaboration or outreach. Time is related to school organization—some of the strategies already mentioned, such as requesting a different schedule, can help with this issue.

THE EFFECTIVENESS OF
ONLINE NETWORKS

It may have come to your attention that use of technology to network has been discussed as a secondary strategy for networking. This is because new teachers often need the most support from their own school; online support networks that focus broadly across a number of contexts can seem irrelevant if they don't address the particular concerns of a teacher. This is not to say that technology is not a great tool for developing networks. However, teachers need to use the technology with what we know about teacher networks in mind. First, teachers may benefit most from developing online relationships and outreach with teachers, parents, and community members from their own school or school district. Second, teachers should develop the type of online professional relationships that meet their needs as teachers; Intentional Professional Networks and Diverse Professional Allies can exist online as well. Third, and finally, use the online tools as a way to share expertise and collaborate. Appendix C of this book includes a resource section of applications and programs that can assist new teachers in fostering online networks. Additionally, new teachers can go online to participate in the companion Web site's online network to discuss their experiences in developing support networks and share ideas for successful online and face-to-face network-building strategies.

NETWORKING TIP

Share your experiences in networking for support, or read about others' efforts at our online community, www.thenetworkedteacher.com/#!community

STRATEGIES FOR SUPPORTING
NEW TEACHERS

The aim of this book is to help new teachers take active, informed stances in developing support networks. Armed with frameworks for understanding what high-quality support looks like, and how social networks function to support teachers, beginning teachers can begin to take steps to seek collaborations and relationships that meet their needs and help to improve their practice. The strategies in this chapter offer a range of options for new teachers to use in developing their network. There are also strategies that the people and institutions that support new teachers can take to assist them in their networking journey.

Teacher educators are first to influence future teachers, and they can guide pre-service teachers to practice networking strategies during their student teaching. Some teacher education programs have begun to consider the role of the community in teaching. For example, at the University of Pennsylvania, student teachers interview community leaders, spend time in the neighborhood, and develop a profile of their school's community for part of their final thesis (Baldino Bonnet, 2006). However, this practice is far from commonplace. Teacher educators need to spend more time helping students learn to navigate the social dynamics of school and building a relationship with the community.

Another individual who often has a strong impact on the experience of a new teacher is a mentor. Many school districts assign mentors, yet often the mentors focus on staying on course with a scripted curriculum or looking at test scores. However, this is precisely the behavior that turns new teachers away from their members, to seek support from less formal support people. Mentors are most helpful to new teachers when they focus on teachers' questions and inquiries and reflect professional support. The Continuum of New Teacher Support also shows that frequent visits (more than once a month) over the year can establish a strong support relationship. Further, mentors can help teachers develop their network by assisting them in examining their support network and strategizing how to build the network. In this case, a mentor based at a school may be the most effective because he or she knows the social dynamics and culture of the school.

School leaders and administrators also have a good understanding of the school culture and can take steps to make the culture, organization, and ideology more network-friendly. To shift the culture, leaders can share the research and framework on social networks with their faculty and be explicit in support of network development. This action increases the faculty's *expertise transparency*—what faculty members know about the knowledge and resources that other faculty have the potential to share (Baker-Doyle & Yoon, 2010). Organizationally, leaders can develop schedules that allow time for teacher collaboration and small learning groups. Leaders should also keep an eye out for the people who could be boundary crossers and teachers with content expertise, and offer opportunities for new teachers to work with them. Finally, ideologically, a school that focuses on improving teaching (the process of teaching) rather than simply improving test scores will be more effective in supporting network development.

Inside and outside of school, formal teacher networks and professional organizations exist to support teachers. Groups that reflect high-quality professional support can be extremely helpful for new teachers in developing their support networks. These groups should be aware of the importance of contextualized support and find ways to link teachers with others who are teaching in either the same school or a school with similar characteristics. Further, context can be similar in subject or pedagogical interests— developing sub-networks for teachers around specific subjects or practices can be helpful for new teachers. Professional organizations can be especially advantageous for teachers who face challenges in developing networks at their own school and in their school communities; offering specific support to such teachers would be of great benefit to them.

NETWORKING FOR SUPPORT

Relationships are complex and messy. They are unique in every context and difficult to predict. For many years, the realm of the classroom and teachers' lives were considered a "black box" to researchers because of this "messiness" problem—it seemed that choices and decisions made by teachers had no logic, rhyme, or reason, or, at least, the rhyme and reason belonged solely to the teachers and was therefore too difficult to measure on a comprehensive scale. Yet, this is the age of the network; relationships matter and are now recognized as integral to the induction of a new teacher, the implementation of policies or curriculum, and the ability of teachers to do their jobs well. This is evident in the plethora of mentoring programs, professional learning communities, and teacher networks that have been formally integrated into schools today to support teachers, new and experienced.

Relationships are messy; however, we (researchers, teachers, administrators, and policymakers) must understand how they work, and what they do, if we are to rely on them to such a great extent in this new age. Although the prospect of understanding the functioning of relationships, networks, and social capital is daunting, it is not impossible. There are characteristics of social capital and social networks that apply to the lives of teachers. There are also identifiable features of support that relate to patterns of teacher learning and experience. As I have described here, Intentional Professional Networks, which are local, professional support relationships developed through active collaboration, can help new teachers to socialize, develop a voice in the school, and gain a sense of teacher identity. Diverse Professional Allies, the parents, students, and community members that are not often recognized as support people, can help new teachers be innovative and more student-centered in their curriculum development.

The stories in this book illustrate the substantial impact of social networks in the lives of new teachers and highlight the ways that Intentional Professional Networks and Diverse Professional Allies offered support to these teachers. However, Michael, Maria, Susan, and Steven often realized the value of these networks as they went through their first year. Readers of this book have the advantage of understanding the theory and research behind social networks and the tools to be a Networked Teacher.

In concluding this book, I have a secret to admit: Networking is challenging for me. I have always been a bit shy, and I used to avoid chatting with others. However, my research on teachers' networks has been transformative for me, as I hope it will be for my readers. Since my work in this area, I have consciously pushed myself to examine my own support networks, collaborate with others, and learn about the community in which I work, just as I urge new teachers to do. The friends and colleagues I have developed through this effort have been invaluable to my work. As our "Network Society" grows in reliance on online and face-to-face networks, the principles of network theory and the stories of new teachers described here may offer a guide and incentive for new teachers to consciously work to build strong, effective support networks of their own.

A Quick Overview of Social Networking Strategies

Identifying Needs and Context

▶ Learn about the school's culture, organization, and ideological approach to teaching.

▶ Reflect on major challenges:
  • Socializing, school politics, isolation → Develop stronger Intentional Professional Networks
  • Curriculum, identity, student relationships → Develop stronger Diverse Professional Allies
  • If multiple challenges, focus on one critical incident

Uncovering the Social Network

▶ List all people who support the teacher in their work.

▶ Describe network members:
  • Demographics
  • Type of relationship to the teacher (friend, colleague, administrator, etc.)
  • Location (at school, in community, outside of community, etc.)
  • Intensity of support they provide
  • Type of support they provide

▶ Examine the network trends:
  • Who offers the most intense support? What type of support do they offer?
  • Look for Intentional Professional Networks (local colleagues providing professional support) and Diverse Professional Allies (nontraditional support persons such as parents, community members)
  • Who offers the least support?
  • Is the teacher involved in any support groups?
  • Any network type missing?
  • Look for connections between challenges and network patterns and identify gaps in the network

Developing Intentional Professional Networks

▶ Action:
  - Collaborate with other teachers using inquiry methods (based on the teachers' practice and questions)
  - Learn from teachers that support inquiry (observe, converse)

▶ Participate:
  - Join formal groups in the school (for example, committees)
  - Join or create non-school-related groups with colleagues (for example, book clubs)
  - Join formal professional networks

Developing Diverse Professional Allies

▶ Presence:
  - Spend time in the community (after school, summertime)
  - Work with local community organizations

▶ Family-centered curriculum:
  - Get to know family's funds of knowledge
  - Center curriculum on family experiences, interests

▶ Broadcasting:
  - Newsletters
  - Use of technology and online networks
  - Show off

Facing Potential Challenges

▶ School culture, organization, or ideology

▶ Tension with parents/lack of community knowledge

▶ Teacher personality

▶ Time

Mapping Tools and Diagrams

List the individuals you go to when you need teaching support:	Describe each person and the kind of support that they offer:

Use the diagram below to map out your support network:

- Octagon: In Intentional Professional Network
- Diamond: In Diverse Professional Ally Network
- Triangle: Offers limited or Traditional support

Draw lines between individuals to indicate if they also seek each other for support. Add or ignore shapes depending on your network.
In examining your map, consider these questions:

- How would you characterize your network overall? Is it dense? Full of cliques? Balanced or imbalanced in some way? Have you sensed an impact in your teaching experience based on the characteristics of the network?
- How many people do you rely on for support inside or outside of your school?

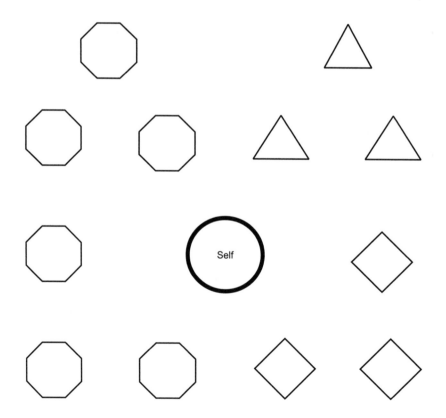

- How does your Intentional Professional Network look?
- How does your Diverse Professional Ally Network look? Are there others linked to them?
- Are there certain networks or characteristics that you think should be developed?

APPENDIX C

Collaborative Technologies

There is a range of technological resources that teachers can use to extend their outreach and collaboration. Documenting and Broadcasting tools can be helpful for teachers who would like to develop their Diverse Professional Ally networks because they provide a public venue for activities in the classroom. Collaboration tools can be helpful to teachers who are designing curricula or programs—and these actions help to build Intentional Professional Networks. In some instances, teachers need additional resources outside of school—especially when they face networking challenges in their schools. Information and friend-seeking tools can assist teachers to reach beyond their schools for support.

DOCUMENTING AND BROADCASTING

Web 1.0

Web 1.0 sites are traditional Web sites or sharing sites that do not allow viewers to comment on or interact with the site. Teachers who would like to share what they are doing in the classroom or with other teachers can post videos, pictures, or writing on these sites, and they do not need to worry about keeping an eye out for inappropriate or spam comments on the site. Examples of this type of site can be viewed at the Carnegie Foundation's Inside Teaching Project, which posts a variety of teachers' inquiry projects online, including videos, pictures, and work samples from students (Pointer-Mace, 2009): http://gallery.carnegiefoundation.org/insideteaching/.

Web 2.0

Web 2.0 sites allow viewers to comment, share, and interact with the site. These include blogs, vlogs, and wikis. A blog is like an online journal. The author writes an entry, or "post," and viewers can comment on the post. Some blogs have multiple authors. Many blog-hosting services are free and

very easy to set up. An example of a popular teacher's blog is: http://cool
catteacher.blogspot.com/ (Davis, 2010). A vlog is a video blog—people post
videos instead of text or pictures in vlogs.

A wiki is a Web site that allows visitors to add to or change it. Think
of it as a word-processing document that anyone can add to or edit. The
most famous wiki is Wikipedia, which is an online encyclopedia created
and edited by the public. Examples of teachers' uses of a wiki can be found
at http://educationalwikis.wikispaces.com/. Like blogs, wikis are often free
and easy to set up. Teachers can use wikis to share news with parents or
other community members or to collaborate with other teachers.

COLLABORATING

Online Social Networks

Perhaps the most well-known online social network is Facebook, which
allows individuals to identify and communicate with "friends" through an
interactive platform. In addition to online software, teachers can use hard-
ware, such as electronic books and phones, to extend their communication.
Teachers can use Facebook as a simple way to keep connected online, but if
they want to be more targeted in their online networking, they can set up a
Ning, which is an online network platform dedicated to only one community or for people interested in a particular topic. One good example of an
educational organization that has successfully used a Ning is the NCTE. The
NCTE created a Ning for attendees of their annual conference, and it has
continued to be a site of networking and collaboration for many members.
You can visit the site at http://ncte2008.ning.com. Finally, for people who
don't have a lot of time, but want to be part of a network, Twitter allows
users to post short statements or links (up to 140, called *tweets*). Visitors
can become "followers" of your site and will receive tweets from you and
can comment on your tweets through their own Twitter accounts.

Project Collaboration Tools

Teachers who need to work on a project with colleagues, but have little time
outside of tools, have a plethora of options for online project collaboration.
Many tools offer the ability to store files and documents, make changes,
and communicate updates. Two examples of free tools for this type of collaboration are Google or Yahoo groups, which create listservs of members,
provide storage for files, and allow members to post messages to the group.
A more complex tool is Basecamp, which can assign tasks to individuals

and set a calendar or schedule for goals in addition to the tools available in Google and Yahoo groups. A virtual learning environment, such as Moodle, which is free and very flexible, can allow similar capabilities and even more creativity on the part of the designer, because it allows the designer to create specific modules for tasks. For simple file-sharing, a program such as Dropbox can place a folder on your computer that is accessible by anyone you allow into the Dropbox network. These collaboration tools can be very helpful in extending conversations and work that begin in school.

Distance Communication

Teachers that need to communicate across long distances now have a range of tools that allow for high levels of interactivity. Skype is a free video-over-Internet tool that allows users to chat or call anyone else on its network. There are also many chat and iVideo programs embedded in online email programs now, such as Google mail and Yahoo mail.

INFORMATION AND FRIEND-SEEKING

With all the Internet sites out there, it can be difficult to sift through them all and find one that is appropriate for your needs. My recommendation is to visit the Web sites of professional organizations and formal teacher networks for links to message boards and information. In addition to the NCTE site, the National Writing Project offers a range of support for literacy teachers. For teachers of other subjects or generalists, one example of an online teacher-support network to investigate is Tappedin.org (Schlager, Farooq, Fusco, Schank, & Dwyer, 2009), which provides a virtual office to members and allows members to travel through the site as if on a college campus. This virtual world idea employed by TappedIn is modeled off of Second Life, a large virtual world program in which members create avatars of themselves and "travel" through the program, meeting and interacting with others along the way.

References

Adams, J. E. (2000). *Taking charge of the curriculum: Teacher networks and curriculum implementation.* New York: Teachers College Press.

Adler, P. S., & Kwon, S. (2002). Social capital: Prospects for a new concept. *Academy of Management Journal, 27*(1), 17–40.

Anderson, L. (2010). Embedded and emboldened: Support-seeking and teacher agency in urban, high-needs schools. *Harvard Educational Review, 80*(4), 541–572.

Anheier, H., Gerhards, J., & Romo, F. P. (1995). Forms of capital and social structure in cultural fields: Examining Bourdieu's social topography. *American Journal of Sociology, 100*(4), 859–903.

Baker-Doyle, K. (2008). *Circles of support: New urban teachers' social support networks.* Retrieved from Proquest (Paper AAI3309395).

Baker-Doyle, K. (2010). Beyond the labor market paradigm: A social network perspective on teacher recruitment and retention. *Education Policy Analysis Archives, 18*(26). Retrieved November 2010, from http://epaa.asu.edu/ojs/article/view/836/863

Baker-Doyle, K. (in press). The social networks of new teachers: Locating and building professional support. *The New Educator.*

Baker-Doyle, K., & Yoon, S. (2010). In search of practitioner-based social capital: A social network analysis tool for understanding and facilitating teacher collaboration in a US-based professional development program. *Professional Development in Education, 37*(1), 75–93.

Baker-Doyle, K., & Yoon, S. (2010). Making expertise transparent: Using technology to strengthen social networks in teacher professional development. In A. J. Daly (Ed.), *Social network theory and educational change* (pp. 115–127). Cambridge: Harvard University Press.

Baldino Bonnet, J. (2006). Seeing with new eyes. *Penn GSE Magazine, Fall,* 8–14.

Bidwell, C., & Yasumoto, J. Y. (1999). The collegial focus: Teaching fields, collegial relationships, and instructional practice in American high schools. *Sociology of Education, 72*(4), 234–256.

Borgatti, S. P., & Foster, P. C. (2003). The network paradigm in organizational research: A review and typology. *Journal of Management, 29*(6), 991–1013.

Boyd, D., Grossman, P., Lankford, H., Loeb, S., & Wycoff, J. (2006). How changes in entry requirements alter the teacher workforce and affect student acheivement. *Education Finance and Policy, 1*(2), 176–216.

Boyd, D., Lankford, H., Loeb, S., & Wycoff, J. (2003). *The draw of home: How teachers' preferences for proximity disadvantage urban schools.* Cambridge, MA: National Bureau of Economic Research.

Brown, J. S., & Duguid, P. (2001). Knowledge and organization: A social practice perspective. *Organization Science, 12*(2), 198–213.

Burns-Thomas, A. (2007). Supporting new visions for social justice teaching: The potential for professional development networks. *Penn GSE Perspectives on Urban Education, 5*(1). Retrieved May 2008, from http://www.urbanedjournal .org/articles/article0031.html

Burt, R. S., & Minor, M. J. (1983). *Applied network analysis: A methodological introduction.* Beverly Hills: Sage Publications.

Carmichael, P., Fox, A., McCormick, R., Proctor, R., & Honour, L. (2006). Teachers' networks in and out of school. *Research Papers in Education, 21*(2), 217–234.

Castells, M. (1996). *The information age: Economy, society and culture. Volume 1: Rise of the network society.* Cambridge, UK: Blackwell Publishing.

Castells, M. (2000). Toward a sociology of the network society. *Contemporary Sociology, 29*(5), 693–699.

Christiansen, H., & Ramadevi, S. (2002). Community and community building in teacher education. In H. Christiansen & S. Ramadevi (Eds.), *ReEducating the educator: global perspectives on community building* (pp. 3–16). Albany: State of New York Press.

Coburn, C. (2001). Collective sensemaking about reading: How teachers mediate reading policy in their professional communities. *Educational Evaluation and Policy Analysis, 23*(2), 145–170.

Coburn, C., Choi, L., & Mata, W. (2010). "I would go to her because her mind is math": Network formation in the context of a district-based mathematical reform. In A. J. Daly (Ed.), *Social network theory and educational change* (pp. 33–50). Cambridge, MA: Harvard Education Press.

Cochran-Smith, M., & Lytle, S. (1993). *Inside/outside: Teacher research and knowledge.* New York: Teachers College Press.

Coleman, J. S. (1987). Families and schools. *Educational Researcher, 16*(6), 32–38.

Coleman, J. S. (1990). *Foundations of social theory.* Cambridge, MA: The Belknap Press of Harvard University Press.

Costigan, A. T., Crocco, M. S., & Zumwalt, K. K. (2004). *Learning to teach in an age of accountability.* Mahwah, NJ: Laurence Erlbaum Associates.

Cross, R., Parker, A., Prusak, L., & Borgatti, S. P. (2003). Knowing what we know: Supporting knowledge creation and sharing in social networks. In R. Cross, A. Parker, & L. Sasson (Eds.), *Networks in the knowledge economy* (pp. 209–231). New York: Oxford University Press.

Daly, A. (2010a). Mapping the terrain: Social network theory and educational change. In A. J. Daly (Ed.), *Social network theory and educational change* (pp. 1–16). Cambridge, MA: Harvard University Press.

Daly, A. (Ed.). (2010b). *Social network theory and educational change*. Cambridge, MA: Harvard Education Press.

Daly, A. J., Finnigan, K. S., & Bolivar, J. M. (2009, April 13–17). *The ebb and flow of network ties: Evolution of a district leadership team*. Paper presented at the American Educational Research Association Conference, San Diego, CA.

Darling-Hammond, L., & McLaughlin, M. W. (1995). Policies that support professional development in an era of reform. *Phi Delta Kappan. 76*(8), 596–604.

Darling-Hammond, L., & Sykes, G. (2003). Wanted: A national teacher supply policy for education: The right way to meet the "highly qualified teacher" challenge. *Education Policy and Analysis Archives, 11*(33), Retrieved June 2005, from http://epaa.asu.edu/ojs/issue/view/11

Davis, V. (2010). Cool cat teacher blog. Retrieved September 2008, from http://coolcatteacher.blogspot.com

Engestrom, Y., Engestrom, R., & Vahaaho, T. (1999). When the center does not hold: The importance of knotworking. In S. Chaiklin, M. Hedegaard, & U. J. Jensen (Eds.), *Activity theory and social practice: Cultural-historical approaches* (pp. 345–374). Aarhus, Denmark: Aarhus University Press.

Feiman-Nemser, S., Schwille, S., Carver, C., & Yusko, B. (1999). *A conceptual review of literature on new teacher induction*. (No. ED449147). Washington, DC: National Partnership for Excellence and Accountability in Teaching.

Frank, K. A., Zhao, Y., & Borman, K. (2004). Social capital and the diffusion of innovations within organizations: The case of computer technology in schools. *Sociology of Education, 77*(April), 148–171.

Freire, T., Henderson, J. V., & Kuncoro, A. (2010). Aid, social capital and village public goods: after the tsunami. MPRA Paper. Retrieved August 26, 2010, from http://mpra.ub.uni-muenchen.de/23877/

Gallucci, C. (2003). Communities of practice and the mediation of teachers' responses to standards-based reform. *Education Policy Analysis Archives, 11*(35). Retrieved July 2005, from http://epaa.asu.edu/epaa/v11n35

Gladwell, M. (2002). *The tipping point: how little things can make a big difference*. Boston: Back Bay.

Granovetter, M. (1985). Economic action and social structure: The problem of embeddedness. *American Journal of Sociology, 91*(3), 481–510.

Granovetter, M. (2003). The strength of weak ties. In R. Cross, A. Parker, & L. Sasson (Eds.), *Networks in the knowledge economy* (pp. 109–129). New York: Oxford University Press.

Hakkarainen, K., Palonen, T., Paavola, S., & Lehtinen, E. (2004). *Communities of networked expertise: Professional and educational perspectives*. Amsterdam, Netherlands: Elsevier.

Hargreaves, A. (2000). Professionals and parents: Personal adversaries or public allies? *Prospects, XXX*(2), 201–213.

Hargreaves, A., Earl, L., Moore, S., & Manning, S. (2001). *Learning to change: Teaching beyond subjects and standards.* San Francisco: Jossey-Bass.

Hausman, C. S., & Goldring, E. B. (2001). Sustaining teacher commitment: The role of professional communities. *Peabody Journal of Education, 76*(2), 30–51.

Haythornthwaite, C. (1996). Social network analysis: An approach and technique for the study of information exchange. *Library and Information Science Review, 18,* 323–342.

Hinds, P. J., Carley, K. M., Krackhardt, D., & Wholey, D. (2000). Choosing work group members: Balancing similarity, competence, and familiarity. *Organizational Behavior and Human Decision Processes, 81*(2), 226–251.

Hollingsworth, S., Dybdahl, M., & Minarik, L. T. (1993). By chart and chance and passion: The importance of relational knowing in learning to teach. *Curriculum Inquiry, 23*(1), 5–35.

Howard, G. R. (1999). *We can't teach what we don't know: White teachers, multiracial schools.* New York: Teachers College Press.

Ingersoll, R., & Smith, T. M. (2003). The wrong solution to the teacher shortage. *Educational Leadership, 60*(8), 30.

Ingersoll, R., & Smith, T. M. (2004). Do teacher induction and mentoring matter? *NASSP Bulletin, 88*(638). Retrieved from http://www.gse.upenn.edu/faculty_research/docs/DoTeacherInductionAndMentoringMatter-2004.pdf

Johnson, S. M., & Birkeland, S. (2003). The schools that teachers choose. *Educational Leadership, 60*(8), 20–24.

Kagan, D. M. (1992). Professional growth among preservice and beginning teachers. *Review of Educational Research, 62*(2), 129.

Kardos, S. M., Johnson, S. M., Peske, H. G., Kauffman, D., & Liu, E. (2001). Counting on colleagues: New teachers encounter the professional cultures of their schools. *Educational Administration Quarterly, 37*(2), 250–290.

Isham, J., Kolodinsky, J., & Kimberly, G., (2004). Effects of volunteering for nonprofit organizations on social capital formation: Evidence from a statewide survey. *Middlebury College Working Paper Series, 3*(05R). Middlbury, VA: Middlebury College.

Krebs, V. (2010). *About Orgnet.com.* Retrieved July 2005, from http://orgnet.com/about.html

Lave, J., & Wenger, E. (1991). *Situated learning: Legitimate peripheral participation.* Cambridge, UK: University of Cambridge Press.

Lawrence-Lightfoot, S. (2003). *The essential conversation.* New York: Random House.

Lee, V. E., Bryk, A. S., & Smith, J. B. (1993). The organization of effective secondary schools. In L. Darling-Hammond (Ed.), *Review of research in education* (Vol. 19, pp. 171–267). Washington, DC: American Educational Research Association.

Lieberman, A. (1995). Practices that support teacher development. *Phi Delta Kappan*, 76(8), 591–596.

Lieberman, A. (2000). Networks as learning communities: Shaping the future of teacher development. *Journal of Teacher Education*, 51(3), 221–227.

Lieberman, A., & Miller, L. (1999). *Teachers—transforming their world and their work*. New York: Teachers College Press.

Lieberman, A., & Wood, D. R. (2003). *Inside the National Writing Project: Connecting network learning and classroom teaching*. New York: Teachers College Press.

Lin, N. (1999). Social networks and status attainment. *Annual Review of Sociology*, 25, 467–487.

Lin, N. (2001). Building a network theory of social capital. In N. Lin, K. Cook, & R. S. Burt (Eds.), *Social capital: Theory and research* (pp. 1–30). New York: Aldine De Gruyter.

Little, J. W. (1990). The mentor phenomenon and the social organization of teaching. *Review of Research in Education*, 16, 297–351.

Little, J. W. (2001). Professional development in pursuit of reform. In A. Lieberman & L. Miller (Eds.), *Teachers caught in the action: Professional development that matters* (pp. 23–44). New York: Teachers College Press.

McCormick, R., Fox, A., Carmichael, P., & Proctor, R. (2010). *Researching and understanding educational networks*. London: Routledge.

Montano, T., & Burstein, J. H. (2006). Learning from las maestras: Experienced teacher activists who remain in the classroom. *Journal of Borderland Education*, 1(1), 29–39.

Moolenaar, N. (2010). *Ties with potential: Nature, antecedents, and consequences of social networks in school teams*. Amsterdam: Netherlands Organisation for Scientific Research.

Musial, D. (1999). Schools as social-capital networks: A new vision for reform. *The Educational Forum*, 63(Winter), 113–120.

Nardi, B., Whittaker, S., & Schwartz, H. (2000). It's not what you know, it's who you know: Work in the information age. *First Monday*, 5(5), http://firstmonday.org/issues/issue5_5/nardi/index.html

Nardi, B., Whittaker, S., & Schwartz, H. (2002). NetWORKers and their activity in intensional networks. *Computer Supported Cooperative Work*, 11, 205–242.

National Center for Educational Statistics (NCES). (2005), *Common Core of Data: Public school data*. Retrieved January 2006, from http://nces.ed.gov

National Commission on Teaching and America's Future (NCTAF). (2003). *No dream denied: A pledge to America's children*. (Vol. 2003). Washington, DC: Author.

Nieto, S. (2003). What keeps new teachers going? *Educational Leadership*, 60(8), 14–18.

Oakes, J., Franke, M. L., Quartz, K. H., & Rogers, J. (2002). Research for high-quality urban teaching: Defining it, developing it, assessing it. *Journal of Teacher Education*, 53(3), 228–234.

Patton, S. (2005). Who knows whom, and who knows what. *CIO Magazine*. Retrieved July 2005, from http://www.cio.com/article/6956/Social_Network_Analysis_Helps_Maximize_Collective_Smarts

Penuel, W. R., & Riel, M. (2007). The "new" science of networks and the challenge of school change. *Phi Delta Kappan, April*, 611–615.

Penuel, W. R., Riel, M., Krause, A. E., & Frank, K. A. (2009). Analyzing teachers' professional interactions in a school as social capital: A social network approach. *Teachers College Record, 111*(1), 124–163.

Pointer-Mace, D. H. (2009). *Teacher practice online: Sharing wisdom, opening doors.* New York: Teachers College Press.

Putnam, R. D. (1995). Bowling alone: America's declining social capital. *Journal of Democracy, 6*, 65–78.

Rowan, B. (1990). Committment and control: Alternative strategies for the organization and design of schools. *Review of Research in Education, 16*, 353–389.

Safer, M. (2007). *The "Millenials" are coming.* CBS News. Retrieved June 2008, from http://www.cbsnews.com/stories/2007/11/08/60minutes/main3475200.shtml

Saronson, S. (1971). *The culture of school and the problem of change.* Boston: Allyn & Bacon.

Schlager, M. S., Farooq, U., Fusco, J., Schank, P., & Dwyer, N. (2009). Analyzing online teacher networks. *Journal of Teacher Education, 60*(1), 86–100.

Spillane, J. P. (1999). External reform initiatives and teachers' efforts to reconstruct their practice: the mediating role of teachers' zones of enactment. *Journal of Curriculum Studies, 31*(2), 143–175.

Spillane, J. P. (2000). A fifth grade teacher's reconstruction of mathematics and literacy teaching: Exploring interactions among identity, learning, and subject matter. *The Elementary School Journal, 100*(4), 307–330.

Spillane, J. P., Halverson, R., & Diamond, J. B. (2004). Towards a theory of leadership practice: a distributed perspective. *Journal of Curriculum Studies, 36*(1), 3–34.

Spillane, J. P., & Thompson, C. L. (1997). Reconstructing conceptions of local capacity: The local education agency's capacity for ambitious instructional reform. *Educational Evaluation and Policy Analysis, 19*(2), 185.

Stone, C. R., & Wehlage, G. G. (1994). Social capital, community collaboration and the restructuring of schools. In F. Rivera-Batiz (Ed.), *Reinventing urban education: Multiculturalism and the social context of schooling.* Ephrata, PA: Science Press.

Strieb, L. (2010). *Inviting families into the classroom: Learning from a life in teaching.* New York: Teachers College Press.

Tellez, K. (1992). Mentors by choice, not design: Help-seeking by beginning teachers. *Journal of Teacher Education, 43*(3), 214–221.

Thomas, A. (2007). Teacher attrition, social capital, and career advancement: An unwelcome message. *Research and Practice in Social Sciences, 3*(1), 19–47.

Wasserman, S., & Faust, K. (1994). *Social network analysis*. New York: Cambridge University Press.

Webster, C. (1995). Detecting context-based contraints in social perceptions. *Journal of Quantitative Anthropology, 5*(4), 285–303.

Weiss, E. M. (1999). Perceived workplace conditions and first-year teachers' morale, career choice commitment, and planned retention: a secondary analysis. *Teaching and Teacher Education, 15*(8), 861–879.

Wellman, B. (1983). Network analysis: Some basic principals. *Sociological Theory, 1*, 155–200.

Wong, H. K., & Wong, R. T. (2008, January 1–7). *Teachers: The Next Generation*. ASCD Express Article.

Yasumoto, J. Y., Uekawa, K., & Bidwell, C. E. (2001). The collegial focus and high school students' achievement. *Sociology of Education, 74*(3), 181–209.

Index

Note: Page numbers followed by "f" refer to figures; those followed by "t" denote tables.

About the Author

Kira J. Baker-Doyle is an assistant professor at Pennsylvania State University–Berks. Her scholarly interests include teacher induction and professional development, teachers' social networks, and urban education. She is currently developing an urban teacher and leader pipeline program with colleagues at Penn State and several Reading, Pennsylvania, community organizations. She is also the principal investigator of the Linking Instructors' Networks of Knowledge in Science Education (LINKS-Ed) project. Dr. Baker-Doyle teaches courses in literacy education and urban education. Prior to academia, she had experience working as an educator and as a businesswoman; she taught elementary grades in the Philadelphia public schools and co-founded a nationally recognized gourmet food company, John & Kira's, with her husband, John Doyle.